Jossey-Bass Guides
to Online Teaching and Learning

Creating a Sense of Presence in Online Teaching

HOW TO "BE THERE" FOR DISTANCE LEARNERS

Rosemary M. Lehman
Simone C. O. Conceição

JOSSEY-BASS
A Wiley Imprint
www.josseybass.com

Published by Jossey-Bass

A Wiley Imprint

989 Market Street, San Francisco, CA 94103-1741—www.josseybass.com

Jossey-Bass books and products are available through most bookstores. To contact Jossey-Bass directly call our Customer Care Department within the U.S. at 800-956-7739, outside the U.S. at 317-572-3986, or fax 317-572-4002.

Jossey-Bass also publishes its books in a variety of electronic formats. Some content that appears in print may not be available in electronic books.

Library of Congress Cataloging-in-Publication Data

Lehman, Rosemary M., 1932-
  Creating a sense of presence in online teaching : how to "be there" for distance learners / Rosemary M. Lehman, Simone C. O. Conceição.
    p. cm. – (Jossey-bass guides to online teaching and learning ; 18)

  Includes bibliographical references and index.
  ISBN 978-0-470-56490-5 (pbk.)
    978-0-470-87309-0 (ebk.)
    978-0-470-87309-0 (ebk.)
    978-0-470-87311-3 (ebk.)

  1. Web-based instruction–Social aspects. 2. Distance education–Social aspects. 3. Education, Higher–Computer-assisted instruction. 4. Human-computer interaction. 5. Emotions and cognition. I. Conceição-Runlee, Simone, 1963- II. Title.
  LB1044.87.L439 2010
  371.35'8–dc22

                                                                2010019253

Printed in the United States of America

FIRST EDITION

PB Printing   10 9 8 7 6 5 4 3 2

CONTENTS

LIST OF FIGURES, EXHIBITS, AND TABLES

FIGURES

EXHIBITS

TABLES

PREFACE

Technology has become omnipresent in our lives. It is with us anytime, anyplace, anywhere; we hardly notice its existence; it has become ubiquitous. Technology brings information to us about what is going on in the world through the palm of our hands and allows us to access that information through the tips of our fingers.

From an educational perspective, technology has given us the opportunity to expand our knowledge and extend our reach to people and places we never considered before. The benefits are beyond our imagination: saving us time, travel, and cost; avoiding the necessity to take risks in going to other locations; allowing us to store information and knowledge and carry them with us wherever we go through mobile devices and other "green" technologies; connecting us to diverse people all over the world and bringing us closer together; allowing us to work in virtual communities that are no longer limited to physical places; and giving us the opportunity to be present with each other without boundaries.

This sense of "being there" with each other in the virtual space often happens informally and spontaneously as part of our everyday lives. But when we try to achieve this sense of being there in formal educational settings, we need a different way of thinking, feeling, and behaving from both an organizational and an instructional perspective. From an organizational perspective, the more structured environment requires that policies and practices be followed for the credential process. From an instructional perspective, it involves planning, intention, and design in order to ensure effective learning outcomes and meet quality standards.

The importance of creating a sense of presence in online teaching and learning environments cannot be overestimated. If you think about the basic difference between learning in the classroom and learning exclusively online, it is the separation of the instructor from the learner and the learners from each other. This separation often leads to feelings of isolation on the part of participants and has been a major cause of learner dissatisfaction in the online learning environment (Palloff & Pratt, 1999).

"Being there" in our book means being present with others in online teaching and learning in a virtual space. But being there in a virtual space in the formal setting doesn't easily happen; rather, the sense of presence needs to be intentionally created. The concept of presence begins with an understanding of our perceptual nature and the influence of the perceptual system on the creation of presence. It is through learner and instructor awareness that presence can be understood and realized. Learner and instructor are psychologically, emotionally, and behaviorally present when they connect with others in an authentic way during the online learning experience. Understanding presence is complex. It requires us to take into consideration the social, psychological, and emotional aspects of presence and the ways in which they influence participants' interactions in the online environment.

Our book provides a model for how to be aware of, think about, and understand creating a sense of presence in the online environment, and it proposes a framework for designing online courses with a sense of presence. Activities that create a sense of presence are described and connected to the model and framework, along with approaches and questions for gathering information on how presence is "there" in online courses.

THE FOCUS OF THIS BOOK

Our book focuses on the need for creating presence in the online environment, explores the concept of presence, and addresses the ways in which the creation of presence can contribute to more interactive online teaching and learning. Based on research and experience, our book provides practical examples through activities, illustrations, and cases that explain how to create, maintain, and evaluate presence throughout an online course.

Our book is based on a learner-centered approach. In this approach, a sense of presence means being there with online learners throughout the learning experience. It looks and feels as if the instructor has placed the learners at the center of the course development and created the course for these learners. It also looks and feels as if the instructor is accessible to the learners and the learners are accessible to the instructor and each other; in addition, the technology is transparent in the learning process. The learner is also involved in the design process by giving feedback and helping shape the online environment.

WHO CAN BENEFIT FROM THIS BOOK

The book offers instructors, instructional designers, and practitioners a guide to becoming aware of the concept of presence. Academics who teach instructional design may use this book as a resource for their courses. Practitioners who work with programs or organizations or as consultants may use this book as a guide when developing online courses or working as consultants assisting educators who create online courses.

HOW THIS BOOK IS ORGANIZED

The first two chapters offer an overview of current research on presence, along with examples. The first four chapters begin and end by following scenarios involving the hypothetical Amanda and Carlos, who illustrate the human experiences of a novice online learner and an inexperienced instructor in the online environment. As the book progresses, both grow and become aware of the importance of presence in the online environment thanks to positive course design and instructor training. These scenarios will help instructors who are new to online teaching and learning cope with their own feelings of insecurity, anxiety, and being overwhelmed in this new venture.

Chapter 1, "The Role of Presence in the Online Environment," discusses why the sense of "being there" and "being together" is so important to online presence; defines the concept of presence and the difference between presence and engagement; and explains the social, psychological, and emotional aspects of presence in the online environment.

Chapter 2, "Ways in Which Presence Can Be Experienced," discusses types of experience, modes of presence, and the dimensions of the learner. These concepts, grounded in perceptual research, help us understand the concept of presence and make up the Being There for the Online Learner model, which we introduce at the end of this chapter.

Chapter 3, "Designing Your Online Course with a Sense of Presence," offers an instructional design framework based on the Being There for the Online Learner model. This framework uses the determinants of presence to design online teaching and learning. Three examples of online courses are presented to illustrate how to use this framework for creating a sense of presence. In addition, the chapter offers an overview of how to get "there" as an instructor and how to get the learners "there" in an online course. Because it is beyond the scope of this book to focus on the design aspects of online teaching and learning, training and design resources are suggested in this chapter.

Chapter 4, "Activities That Create a Sense of Presence in Your Online Course," provides activity examples in the potential sequence in which they may be used (before the course begins, during the course, and at the end of the course). Within each sequence, the chapter explains how to use the determinants of presence and suggests approaches and questions for gathering information to help you know if presence is occurring in the online course.

Chapter 5, "Are You Here or There? Making Sense of Presence," presents three activity case examples. Each one addresses one or more of the three sequences in an online course (before the course, during the course, and at the end of the course). The chapter then provides a sample syllabus that incorporates a sense of presence. It ends with final thoughts and future directions.

ACKNOWLEDGMENTS

Creating this book was a lively and genuine experience of connecting and being present with each other during the writing process. Either face-to-face or online, we worked together combining our knowledge of the field and practical experience. We used a developmental approach for the writing process through continuous brainstorming and frequent feedback from online instructors and learners.

We would like to acknowledge the feedback we received from Brian Altman, Les Johnson, and Steve Schmidt during the early stages of the writing process. We would like to thank Les Johnson for helping us create the first draft of the graphics for the book. We are especially grateful to Vern Mason and Lei Zhang from Union Pacific Media Studio at Michigan State University (http://www.bus. msu.edu/learcenter) for their artistic skills in transforming our two-dimensional concept of the model and framework into three-dimensional graphic designs. We also appreciate Steve Schmidt's contribution of Case 1 in Chapter 5. His experience as an online instructor and adult educator strengthened our book. Our editor, Erin Null, provided invaluable insights, comments, and suggestions during the progress of our work that helped reshape our thinking and writing. She was "present" with us throughout the entire process, giving us highly professional and gracious feedback. To the most important individuals in our lives, our family members—your emotional and psychological support helped the creation process flow smoothly. Our special thanks to Don Lehman, who encouraged us to remain focused throughout our writing.

We hope this book creates an awareness of the importance of the concept of the sense of presence and an understanding of how to apply it in the online environment. The sense of presence can be an elusive concept, but the more we become aware of it and deeply understand it, the easier it will be to make it happen.

Rosemary M. Lehman
Madison, Wisconsin
Simone C. O. Conceição
Milwaukee, Wisconsin

ABOUT THE AUTHORS

Rosemary M. Lehman, Ph.D., is an author and consultant in the field of distance education. For nearly twenty years she worked for the University of Wisconsin-Extension. Most recently, she was the Senior Outreach/Distance Education Specialist at Instructional Communications Systems (ICS), University of Wisconsin-Extension (UWEX), and manager of the ICS Learning Design and Outreach Team, where she supervised the training of faculty and staff in the use of technology for teaching and learning, and taught via technology. She received her doctorate in distance education and adult learning, and her master's in television and media critique, from the University of Wisconsin-Madison. She is the author of *The Essential Videoconferencing Guide: 7 Keys to Success* (2001) and a number of book chapters and journal articles, the editor of *Using Distance Education Technology: Effective Practices* (2002), and the coauthor of *147 Practical Tips for Synchronous and Blended Technology Teaching and Learning* (2007).

Dr. Lehman's research interests include teaching and learning at a distance for all ages; technology accessibility; the relationship of perception, emotion, and cognition to distance learning and instructional design; educational applications for media and technology; and the development and integration of learning objects into learning experiences. She has keynoted and presented at a wide variety of statewide, national, and international conferences and was the recipient of the 2005 University of Wisconsin-Extension Award for Excellence in distance education and leadership.

Simone C. O. Conceição, Ph.D., is an associate professor of adult and continuing education. She teaches courses in the areas of distance education, use of technology with adult learners, instructional design, and principles and foundations of adult learning. She received her doctorate in adult and distance education from the University of Wisconsin-Madison and her master's in adult and continuing leadership education from the University of Wisconsin-Milwaukee. Prior to joining the faculty, she was an instructional design/technology consultant, working with faculty and staff providing training and consultation on instructional design and the use of technology for instruction. She coauthored *147 Practical Tips for Teaching Online Groups: Essentials for Web-Based Education* (2000) and is the editor of *Teaching Strategies in the Online Environment* (2007).

Dr. Conceição's research interests include adult learning, distance education, impact of technology on teaching and learning, instructional design, learning objects, and staff development and training. Born in Brazil, she has lived in the United States since 1989. Her diverse background brings an international perspective to the fields of education and training. She has researched and identified many aspects of good practice in online environments, and she is an expert in helping instructors and trainers understand Web-based technology tools, software, and design processes. She received the 2006 Early Career Award from the Commission of Professors of Adult Education.

Creating a Sense of Presence in Online Teaching

The Role of Presence in the Online Environment

Scenario 1. At thirty-five, Amanda is a newly enrolled learner in an online master's program in adult education. She works full-time for a training and development company, is married, and has a small child. Time is a premium in her life—that's why she chose to enroll in an online program. This is her first experience with online learning, and her technology skills are limited. She is worried about the differences between the face-to-face courses she's so familiar with and the courses she will now be taking. She wonders how she will interact with the instructor and other learners, how she will be able to feel that she belongs to a community of learners and feel that this experience is "real." She is so used to working with trainees on an interactive basis that she cannot imagine how the feeling of "being there" and "being together" with others in this program will be possible. All she can envision is the computer and the books. She is beginning to feel lonely, anxious, and isolated.

Scenario 2. Carlos is a twenty-seven-year veteran instructor at a community college who was recently asked to offer his communications courses online. He is reluctant to do so because his classes are very interactive—they require small-group work, team project presentations, experiential field work, and active discussion. He worries that his years of teaching will be irrelevant. He does not understand how to adapt his course from the face-to-face to the online environment.

1

where is satisfaction
& personal interaction?

He asks himself: *How am I going to develop this course? What will my course feel and look like? How do I connect with my learners and get to know them? How will I adapt and implement the small-group work, team projects, and discussion activities to my online course?* All he can see is the computer and his class materials.

As instructors and designers in the field of online education, we cannot over-estimate the importance of creating a sense of presence in online teaching and learning. Close your eyes and envision for just a minute the basic difference between learning face-to-face and learning exclusively online. Even before the minute is up, it will likely be obvious to you that the basic difference is the separation between the instructor and the learner and between the learners and each other. This separation naturally leads to feelings of isolation on the part of instructors and learners alike and has been a major reason for learner dissatisfaction and lack of retention in the online learning environment (Palloff & Pratt, 1999), as suggested by Amanda's scenario at the beginning of this chapter. The feeling of isolation is due to a lack of awareness and understanding of the concept of presence. In scenario 2, Carlos, the inexperienced online instructor, needs to be aware of and understand the concept of presence in order to effectively adapt his course to this new environment and feel a connection with his learners.

dissatisfaction
poor retention

WHY IS IT IMPORTANT TO UNDERSTAND PRESENCE?

The Internet is a social space. Today, Internet technology is ever-present, com-pletely woven into our lives. We accomplish many of our communications and transactions via the Web without even noticing. As a result of this omnipresent feeling, we tend to want to be together with others even though we can't see them. These feelings of wanting to be together with others are often expressed through Internet-based social networking tools.

As Internet-based technology evolves in this social direction, it points to the importance of the sense of presence. To create presence in the online environ-ment, we need to think, feel, and behave differently than we do in the face-to-face environment because we have to make an effort to be aware of the intentions of others and their thoughts, emotions, and behaviors when they are connected to us via technology (Biocca, Burgoon, Harms, & Stoner, 2001). When we become aware of and understand the differences between in-person and online interactions, we are better able to select appropriate technology and design learning environments that help create a sense of presence.

In this chapter, we will discuss why creating the sense of *being there* and *being together* is so important for online presence, define the concept of presence and the difference between presence and engagement, and explain the social, psychological, and emotional aspects of presence in the online environment.

CREATING A SENSE OF PRESENCE

Current research shows that when there is a sense of presence in online learning, it can greatly enhance the instructor-learner relationship (Munro, 1998). We agree with this research and believe that this goal can be accomplished. But this belief opens up an array of questions: What is a sense of presence? What does it look and feel like? How is it created? How is presence different from engagement?

What Is a Sense of Presence?

being there
being together with others

Biocca, Burgoon, Harms, and Stoner (2001) discuss the concept of presence as two interrelated phenomena: *telepresence* (the sense of "being there") and *social presence* (the sense of "being together with others," including people, animals, avatars, and so on). Telepresence in the online environment happens when learners have the impression or feeling that they are present at a location remote from their own immediate environment. Social presence means interactions with others in the online environment. We use the terms *being there* and *being together* in this book as the bases for our definition of a sense of presence.

What Does Presence Look and Feel Like?

From our perspective, a sense of presence is "being there" and "being together" with online learners throughout the learning experience. It looks and feels as if the instructor has placed the learner at the center of the course development and created the course for that learner. It also looks and feels as if the instructor is accessible to the learners and that the learners are accessible to the instructor and each other, and that the technology is transparent to the learning process. Each learner is "there" and "together" with the instructor and with other learners as well. Learners are also involved in the design process by giving feedback and

[handwritten margin note: Instructor planning]

helping shape the online environment. In the process, all the T's have been crossed and the I's dotted for this experience. In other words, the instructor has taken into consideration the entire learning experience prior to the course, during the course, and at the end of the course, along with all of the elements that help make presence happen. These elements will be introduced later in this chapter.

How Is Presence Created?

The teaching-learning process for creating presence online may feel overwhelming to those like Carlos who are new to the online environment. But it does not need to be. This book will suggest strategies to decrease these feelings. Still, it is important to know that a sense of presence doesn't just naturally happen. Creating presence is a result of awareness, understanding, involvement through experience, and intentional planning and design on the part of the instructor, the entire support team (that is, instructional designer, technical support, and so on), and the learners who participate in and help negotiate that design. When this process is thoughtfully implemented, the impact on the learners—like Amanda—can be significant. It can create an awareness of what online presence means for them, help them break feelings of isolation, get them involved in the learning process, and bring them together in a virtual community.

[handwritten note: attitude adjust — Validity of virtual community]

How Is Presence Different from Engagement?

Engagement is only one aspect of presence: it is the participation of the instructor with learners or learners with other learners as they interact in the online environment. In contrast, presence includes the dynamic interplay of thought, emotion, and behavior in the online environment. This dynamic interplay takes place both consciously and unconsciously as instructors and learners experience both the real world and the online environment. We believe that presence will not be felt completely until this dynamic interplay has been realized. This book looks at social presence and engagement as aspects of presence rather than presence in its entirety.

WHAT WE KNOW ABOUT PRESENCE

In the current research discussion of presence in the world of online learning, the focus is on creating engagement, a rich environment for learner interaction, and a sense of community, which together result in an enhanced social presence. Garrison, Anderson, and Archer (2001, 2003) describe this enhancement through engagement when they talk about producing a richer social atmosphere and generating a climate for high-level dialogue and critical thinking. Ijsselsteijn, de Ridder, Freeman, and Avons (2000) also address this idea when they speak of creating a sense of the learners and the instructors being together in an online classroom.

The concept of social presence has been extensively addressed in the literature. In Kehrwald's (2008) study, it is defined as "an individual's ability to demonstrate *like* *chat* his/her state of being in a virtual environment and so signal his/her availability for interpersonal transactions" (p. 94). The ability to be social in a virtual space is affected by immediacy, degree of awareness, and willingness to engage in communication exchanges. Immediacy is fundamental to effective interpersonal transactions; the higher the interaction among learners and the instructor, the greater the level of social presence (Tu & McIsaac, 2002). Without participant *needs to* awareness of being perceived as a "real" person ("being there" and "being together") in mediated communications, there is a lack of social presence (Gunawardena & Zittle, 1997). Social presence also means there is a willingness on the part of participants to engage in communication exchanges. This willingness is motivated by purposeful interactions that benefit all. According to Kehrwald (2008), "Motivation is provided by either *need*, as in the case of learning tasks that require interaction, or *interest*, as in the case of relations that motivate ongoing interaction" (p. 97, italics in original).

Tu and McIsaac's (2002) research found that the social context, online communication, and interactivity affect social presence. The social context is created *what are* *if of this?* based on participants' characteristics and their perception of the online environment. Online communication can positively influence social presence when it is stimulating, expressive, carries feelings and emotions, is significant, and is implicit. When interactions among participants are enjoyable, immediate, and reactive, and when participants are comfortable and recognize discussion themes, social presence is positively affected.

According to the research, social presence is central to the creation of effective online learning. Caspi and Blau (2008) have investigated the self-projection of participants onto the group and their identification with the group and found that they positively correlate with each other. They noted that social presence can effectively influence learning by creating a comfortable environment. They also found a positive correlation with aspects of perceived learning.

Moreover, Swan and Shih's (2005) investigation indicates that learners who perceive high social presence during online exchanges also think that they learn more from their interactions with others because they benefit from their ideas. They further suggest that learners may need to be socially engaged with online communities. In order for that to occur, learners need to be introduced to the notion of community building, knowledge construction as a group, and ways of being present during online discussions.

Supplementing the research on social presence and community, Gunawardena (1995) has added the importance of the online learner context. She says that the context in which participants learn and their relationships within that context have an effect on the online learning experience. Lehman (2006) expands on the concepts of social presence, community, and learner context by suggesting the creation of an environment that considers the perceptual nature of the learner. She describes this environment by using what we call a *perceptual systems approach*. This approach considers learners as perceivers who bring their individual knowledge, skills, attitudes, preferences, and diverse backgrounds to the online learning experience. From this perspective, learners are active perceivers, rather than passive receivers, during the entire online learning experience. The perceptual systems approach considers the learner to be central to the online learning experience before, during, and at the end of the course.

PRESENCE AS THE RESULT OF OUR PERCEPTUAL PROCESS

Why is creating presence so important? We are basically social creatures. When the social aspect is absent, we tend to crave it and look for ways to accommodate its absence. Our social nature is integral to our perceptual process when interacting with others not only in the real world but also in the online environment. Through the process of perceiving, we interact with information and others in the online environment, which requires others to relate to us and work with us—this happens at the behavioral level. Individually we make sense of information for our use, for sharing, and for further interacting with others to refine and expand our knowledge. We search for appropriate resources to challenge, support, and enhance our experiences. We then reexamine the entire process by refining what we have integrated, resulting in circling back to repeat the process; this happens at both the cognitive and emotional levels. We continuously go through this process in the online environment from an individual point of view—in other words, perceptually (Lehman, 1996, 2006). Because this process occurs at the subconscious level (Noe, 2005), it is difficult to notice when it is happening.

When thought, emotion, and behavior work together in our real-world experiences, we believe that we have created a successful perceptual experience and a sense of presence. Often we do not realize what happens when we are, for example, assigned to a small group in a face-to-face class (the environment), interacting with group members (with emotion), and focusing, following, and completing the group assignment (with thought, based on group behavior). This perceptual experience parallels the online learning experience, but in the online learning experience the instructor and learners are not in the same physical space. It is therefore necessary to intentionally rethink and redesign the course to incorporate the dynamic interplay of thought, emotion, and behavior so that the perceptual process is influenced and a sense of presence is created in the online environment.

For both Amanda and Carlos, perceptual presence is their sensory experience of "being there" and "being together" with others. It involves their recognition of the online environment and their actions in response to this environment. Through the perceptual process, which involves thought, emotion, and behavior, they interact with information and others and feel as though they are together in this learning experience.

UNDERSTANDING PRESENCE

The concept of presence is complex and not easy to understand. Presence is the result of the dynamic interplay of thought, emotion, and behavior in the online environment, between the private world (that is, the inner world) and the shared world (that is, the outer world) (Garrison & Arbaugh, 2007) and is rooted in the interactive (that is, enactive) perceptual process (Noe, 2005). Therefore, presence should be viewed from different perspectives: social, psychological, and emotional.

The Social Aspect

The first perspective involved in the concept of presence is social presence, a concept that surfaced in the 1970s when Short, Williams, and Christie (1976) wrote about individuals being seen as "real" when communicating using media. They found that the amount of presence was based on the type of media used. For example, distance learners received video cassettes recorded by instructors as a resource to supplement correspondence study. Learners felt a sense of instructor presence when they listened to the instructor's voice and could hear the nuance and tone. Today it is believed that while the type of media used has some influence on social presence in online environments, social presence has more to do with how well individuals participating in online learning are successful in acknowledging or disregarding the presence of the medium (Lombard & Ditton, 1997) and feel that they are together with others (Biocca, Burgoon, Harms, & Stoner, 2001), as previously mentioned.

Garrison, Anderson, and Archer (2003) have incorporated social and teaching presence in their Community of Learning and Inquiry model, viewing these two types of presence as elements of cognitive presence. From their perspective, social presence and teaching presence have to do with how instructor and learners, via online technology, individually and socially see each other as "real people."

Palloff and Pratt (2007) consider social presence to be a critical element in online community building. They say that in online environments there is a greater chance for learners to feel isolated because of a sense of loss of contact and connection with others. Social presence gives learners a feeling of connecting and belonging to a community.

For learners like our hypothetical Amanda, considering the social aspect of presence when designing a course can help reduce feelings of isolation. And if Carlos addresses the social aspect of presence, he can adapt and incorporate group activities that mirror the strategies he uses in his face-to-face course.

The Psychological Aspect

In the second perspective, according to Lombard and Ditton (1997), presence is a psychological state in which the technology becomes transparent to users, who no longer recognize it in the learning experience. In other words, an illusion is created in which the technology seems to disappear and people and locations that are actually separated feel that they are together in the same room.

Simulations are an example of online environments in which technology becomes transparent. Simulations involve the imitation of the real world in the virtual world. The technology creates an illusion of the real world so that the participants no longer perceive the existence of the medium (Lombard & Ditton, 1997).

However, it can be challenging for novice learners and instructors to achieve the feeling of transparency. They may feel anxious and reluctant about the online environment and focus on the technology rather than on the learning experience. After they become psychologically comfortable with the online environment, the technology is no longer a distraction and they have the potential to better experience presence.

We should clarify the term *virtual* as we use it in this book. We use the term in two ways: *virtual space* and *virtual world*. When we refer to the online environment, we are referring to the virtual space in which learners participate in the learning experience. When we use the term virtual world we are referring to a computer-based simulated environment that involves immersive experiences.

The Emotional Aspect

The third perspective, emotional presence, is the ability to genuinely show feelings through words, symbols, and interactions with others in the online environment. In this process, learners and instructors are emotionally present when they connect with others in an authentic way during the online learning experience.

We humans are perceptual by nature, dynamically interacting in the perceptual environment to create representations of our world that allow us to organize information into stories or self-narratives. Our perceptual environment is our awareness of all sensory information (Noe, 2005), which includes a recognition of our own body and inner self. This awareness provides us with information about the external world, the body, and the internal world. Our perceptual process manages and integrates this information, and represents it to us consciously and unconsciously. During this process, emotions affect our behavior and thought and our experience of presence. Emotions are key to perception; they guide us to focus on particular aspects of a situation, enable us to concentrate on that situation, connect the affective to the cognitive, and to arrive at thoughtful and appropriate decisions for our actions (Alcañiz, Bañoa, Botella, & Rey, 2003).

The emotional aspect of presence includes the active process of receiving, responding to, valuing, organizing, and characterizing what is important (Krathwohl, Bloom, & Masia, 1964). Emotions are a kind of gatekeeper for our perceptions and act both with and without the intervention of thought. We need to consider the role of emotion in online learning because it helps us recognize the environment where learning takes place: online interactions among participants and the creation of a learning community.

Environment Where Learning Takes Place   The online environment is often defined based on how an individual observes and perceives something concrete, such as the type of technology used in the course, the type of the learning community formed, the interactive strategies implemented, the role played by the instructor, and the content. These aspects of the online environment are often recognized by instructors when they design face-to-face courses, where emotional cues are easily recognized because of their physical closeness to participants. But in the online environment, they need to be intentionally included in order to create presence.

The concept of presence is rarely considered in the design of an online environment because it is difficult to understand how it will play out in the learning experience. But when a course is designed with presence in mind, the experience comes alive and the learning process is driven by the dynamic interplay between thought, emotion, and behavior.

Online Interactions Among Participants   Technological advances and the use of the Internet in online learning have changed the way we view online interactions among participants. Today these interactions are evolving: life is increasingly virtual as we carry out more and more of our communications and transactions via the Web; instructors increasingly serve as guides and mentors for learners; learners express the desire to be emotionally interconnected with other people even when they can't see them; and feelings of "being there" and behaving socially with other people are expressed through social networking tools. Thus Carlos needs not only to be familiar with the design of online courses but also to be aware of emerging technologies.

These kinds of changes are beginning to lead instructors and designers to rethink how to create online learning environments that are socially interactive, create learning communities, and help learners feel a sense of presence during the online learning experience.

Creation of an Online Learning Community   One way to consider emotion as a guide in the development of presence in online learning communities is to use collaborative and reflective communication among participants. Garrison, Anderson, and Archer (2003) developed the Community of Inquiry Model through the occurrence of three elements that are essential for an online educational experience: cognitive, social, and teaching presence.

- *Cognitive presence* relates to thinking and involves the ability of learners to start, create, and validate meaning through reflection and dialogue in the online environment.

- *Social presence* involves personal and emotional connection to the group. In online environments, individuals are able to express themselves socially and emotionally in a genuine manner if the design of the course is successful. Social presence can facilitate cognitive presence because in order for learners to express their thoughts, ideas, and feelings in the online environment they need to feel comfortable relating to others.

- *Instructor presence* is the voice of the facilitator, who serves as a model for the critical discourse, provides constructive critique, and gives formative feedback. A successful educational experience involves the balance and interaction of cognitive, social, and instructor presence (Garrison, 2003).

There is no question that creating a sense of presence in the online environment is critical. As we already mentioned, people are social beings by nature, and today the Internet is one of our social spaces. Because of the differences between the physical space of the real world and the virtual space, our sense of presence is felt and experienced in different ways. In the physical space, presence is easier to recognize through observation and perception. In the virtual space, presence needs to be intentionally created. The feeling of presence in the virtual space is the result of the dynamic interplay of thought, emotion, and behavior between the private world and the shared world. It is rooted in the interactive perceptual process. While most research focuses on cognitive, social, and teaching presence, this book considers them, but sees a perceptual systems approach as central to the design process. Designing with a sense of presence starts with an awareness of presence and places the learner at the center of the design process.

In the beginning of this chapter, we introduced you to Amanda and Carlos. Amanda did not know why she felt lonely, anxious, and isolated even before her online courses started. Carlos could not imagine how his interactive course could possibly be taught totally online. These two hypothetical cases present the typical concerns of novice learners and inexperienced instructors when working in the online environment. Their feelings of apprehension show how the concept of presence is elusive and hard to grasp when there is an unfamiliarity with this environment. We must take into consideration the social, psychological, and emotional aspects of presence and ways in which they influence participants' interactions in the online community.

SUMMARY

In this chapter we discussed why fostering feelings of "being there" and "being together" are so important in creating online presence, and we provided an overview of the current research on presence. We also defined the concept of presence and explained the difference between presence and engagement, as well as the social, psychological, and emotional aspects of presence in the online environment. In Chapter 2, we will focus on how, according to perceptual research, presence can be experienced in the online environment, and we will introduce you to the Being There for the Online Learner model.

Ways in Which Presence Can Be Experienced

Scenario 1. Amanda has just received the orientation packet for the online course that will start in three weeks. As she opens the packet she feels overwhelmed with the amount of information included and the number of preparatory activities she has to complete before the semester starts. She does not know where to begin. She wonders: *What do I do if I do not understand how to proceed with this packet? Who do I call? Who do I talk to? What other technologies in addition to the computer will I need to use to participate in this course? What will the online class look like? How do I get to know anyone in the online course? Is online really for me?*

Scenario 2. Carlos is scheduled to attend his first professional development and training session on online teaching. He feels like a learner again, this time in an area that is totally foreign to him. He has heard so many conflicting stories about teaching online. Are they true or are they myths? He is very comfortable in the face-to-face classroom but is not sure how the learners will react to his online communications courses. How will he format the learning experience, what interactive strategies will he use with his students, what kind of instructor will he be, what types of technology will he use, and who can he call in for help? He wonders: *Is online teaching really for me? How can I create the same learning experience I provide in the face-to-face classroom?*

Recognizing presence in a face-to-face situation is likely to be relatively easy through observation and perception. After all, we are right there for the interaction. But when we need to experience presence in an environment that is intangible, elusive, and unfamiliar, it is considerably more difficult. Our first reaction is to be skeptical that this can provide a quality experience and to consider this type of learning to be "second-class." There are several reasons why we feel this way: the lack of visual and verbal cues, doubts about the identity of those interacting with us, and unease about feeling impersonal with others. There's also concern about identifying learner differences.

Myths arise. People believe that learners cannot adjust to the online environment; that the instructor does everything in the online course; that course preparation and delivery take less time; that online courses are not good for group interaction and activities; and that online courses are not social in nature. Another myth is that learners will always understand what the instructor expects of them (Hanna, Glowacki-Dudka, & Conceição-Runlee, 2000).

As we saw in the beginning of this chapter, Amanda felt overwhelmed and had many questions about the online environment because she was unfamiliar with online learning. This reaction is typical. Her questions relate to ways in which presence can be experienced online. Carlos's misunderstanding of and discomfort with the online environment result from the conflicting stories he has heard from others. One way for him to become aware of how presence can be experienced in his online course is to understand the types of experiences he can incorporate into his course, the modes of presence, and the dimensions of learners. He took the right first step when he scheduled his professional development and training session.

In this chapter we will discuss ways in which the feeling of presence can be created through types of experience, modes of presence, and learner dimensions. These ways of creating presence are important because they address abstract concepts in a concrete way. Through descriptions and examples of how presence can be experienced in different ways, you will be able to think about how you can incorporate presence into your courses. We will end the chapter by suggesting a Being There for the Online Learner model and how to put it to work in the online environment.

TYPES OF EXPERIENCE

Four types of experience are related to creating a sense of presence: subjective experience, objective experience, social experience, and environmental experience. These types of experiences are based on concepts addressed by Ijsselsteijn, de Ridder, Freeman, and Avons (2000).

Subjective Experience

Subjective experience is personal and psychological presence and takes place in our mind. It is the illusion of being in another location. For example, when our learners are experiencing online learning, they may have the illusion of being in another location as their minds interact with the content, with you (the instructor), and with other learners. The subjective, dynamic interplay that results from this interaction is guided by the learners' emotions, which direct both thought and behavior. This interplay is unique for each learner.

Because Amanda did not know what to expect in the online environment, she felt anxious. To reduce this kind of tension in your learners, you can enhance the feeling of subjective presence by incorporating features and strategies that help convince them that they are with you, psychologically, in their minds. Learners who rarely participate in course interactions cannot yet feel that they are personally and psychologically present in the online environment.

The first step is to create orientation materials that offer activities requiring learners to interact with other learners. Introductory activities that can help learners get to know each other and feel they are personally and psychologically there can encourage subjective experience. Examples of introductory activities will be provided in Chapter 4.

Objective Experience

Objective experience gives you and your learners a sense that you are psychologically and physically in another location (Ijsselsteijn, de Ridder, Freeman, & Avons, 2000). You feel as if you are actually located within the technology-mediated space. Objective experience has occurred in our teaching. Our learners have experienced a feeling of psychologically and physically being in the same space with others during an online class, even though they were separated by thousands of miles. At the end of the semester, learners provided summative feedback and shared that at times they felt as though they were all actually in the same room. They felt close, and the technology became transparent. Our learners were so deeply engaged psychologically and physically during the course interactions that they felt a sense of presence.

At the beginning of this chapter, Amanda was inquiring about who she could call or talk to if she had concerns. One way to address the issue of objective experience for learners like Amanda is to have a help desk contact available via telephone, chat, e-mail, video, or more than one medium. A help desk contact would let Amanda feel that she could be together both psychologically and physically with a staff member to resolve any concerns. As for Carlos, he questioned his ability to teach online and create an experience similar to the one he provides in his face-to-face classroom. Carlos and his learners can benefit from a strategy similar to that used by Amanda. Through Skype he can schedule chat, audio, and video meetings—that is, he can offer electronic office hours. In this way, Carlos and his learners may feel they are together both psychologically and physically in the same location.

To obtain an objective experience, the online course needs to work without distractions and the focus must be on the online learning experience. Other strategies to ensure that the online learning experience runs smoothly include offering clear directions for content activity, providing a well-designed learning experience format so that learners know where and how to post comments, promoting active and balanced participation of group members, making sure that the instructor's presence is evident, having functioning technology, and offering timely support.

Social Experience

Social experience is when everyone in the online environment has a sense of being with the others and respond to each other. Social presence derives from communicating and interacting with others or with animated characters—for example, interacting with avatars in Second Life®, a 3-D virtual world in which learners create an avatar to represent themselves. When learners recognize and respond to one another, it validates both the individual and the group existence. The importance of ongoing interactions is significant and allows and facilitates feelings of understanding (Hargreaves, 2004).

The premise of social presence is simply that if more than one person is in the online environment, there is more evidence that the environment really exists. If others ignore you, you begin to question your own existence (Hawkins & Pingree, 1982). Think of learners who read postings online but do not respond to others. These so-called lurkers do not fully actualize their social presence in the course. The same strategies (that is, small-group work, team project presentations, active discussion) that Carlos uses in his face-to-face course can be used in his online course. However, he needs to adapt them. Such strategies provide opportunities for a learner like Amanda to get to know others in her online course. Examples of these strategies will be addressed in Chapter 4.

Environmental Experience

The ability to easily access and modify (Sheridan, 1992), provide input about, and interact with the online environment is a key element of presence. A description of the environmental experience incorporates both the physical and the educational aspects of the learning experience. The physical aspect involves the learners having technical access and support for the technology and tools they are using. Amanda was anxious about the types of technology she might have to use in addition to her computer—such as audio, video, or handheld devices. If she had technical support available, it would relieve her anxiety.

The educational aspect comprises the instructor's openness and the design of a course structure that allows learners to feel that they are an integral part of the environment and can react to it. This is an area that Carlos must be prepared for before his course begins. Learners' confidence that they have technical access and support, and their feeling that they have an effect on the online course structure, are important in the experience of presence. In the educational aspect of the experience, you should be open to having the learners modify the online environment through challenging preconceived assumptions, providing formative feedback, negotiating the course design with you, determining the team make-up, and creating and sharing projects. The more input from participants to modify the online environment, the greater their feeling of reality and sense of presence. In the environmental experience learners are partners who are central to the design process.

To create presence based on the environmental experience, during the course orientation Carlos needs to communicate to his learners the protocols for technical access and support and the tools they will need to use. Learner feedback about the online environment remains crucial throughout the course. Creating an online forum (that is, the help desk, sharing "almost" anything, and so on) where learners can provide input about the course and assist each other through interactions, is a must.

MODES OF PRESENCE

Ijsselsteijn, de Ridder, Freeman, and Avons (2000) have identified four modes in which we experience presence: realism, immersion, involvement, and suspension of disbelief. We create the "illusion of nonmediation" in each mode so that we no longer perceive the existence of the medium in our communication environment and respond as though the medium were transparent.

Today we use a variety of technologies and tools such as desktop computers, laptop computers, and mobile devices (for example, the iPhone, Blackberry, Palm, iPod Touch, iPad). Because we have become so accustomed to them, they have become transparent in our everyday experiences. They are everywhere and connect us with people and resources in ways previously unimagined. They make us feel as if we are present with each other. When this occurs, it is both a perceptual and a social experience, and it can be a powerful experience. When we participate in an online course that is well designed, we often forget that technology in the learning experience. The boundary between the real and virtual dissolves; the liminal line that initially separated us disappears.

Realism

In realism, there is a close match between the real and the virtual worlds. We try to match as closely as possible the elements of the human senses (vision, hearing, and touch) to those that are used in the online experience in order to replicate the reality (Argyle & Dean, 1965). Nursing simulators are a good example of a realistic experience that closely resembles the actual one. The learner can practice cardiac pulmonary resuscitation (CPR), for example, in a simulated environment that mirrors real-world experience. In a communications course, where the focus is training participants in intercultural communication, a simulation can provide a realistic business context and give learners the opportunity to experience a conflict of cultural values. Here, participants can be divided into several fictional cultures with specific cultural characteristics. This would be a perfect realism activity for Carlos to consider including in his course.

Immersion

In immersion, illusion occurs through virtual reality. The Second Life® 3-D virtual environment is a good example of this mode. Participants experience presence in this virtual world through the creation of avatars. These avatars become their identity and exist in a predesigned environment, immersing themselves in the virtual world. In immersion, illusion is created by detailed mapping to physical reality and vicariously moving around in the virtual environment, interacting with others. Imagine an organizational communications course in which learners are assigned the task of analyzing the way organizations develop their communication plans. Learners can access Second Life® to search for organizations, observe their profiles, and compare and contrast their branding and images. In this example, learners are immersed in the virtual environment by navigating as avatars, interacting with others, and learning through simulated organizations.

Involvement

Involvement creates personal, interactive engagement with the learner and others. Through the design of interactive activities, the line between the real and the virtual world is blurred. For example, think of Amanda as an actively involved participant in an online team project. She engages in dynamic conversations with classmates through synchronous and asynchronous technologies. Her conversations with others become so lively that at times the technology seems to disappear. She senses that she is in the same room with others, but actually she is feeling a sense of presence with others in the online environment.

Suspension of Disbelief

The suspension of disbelief is a psychological "letting go" of reality. In this mode, the participants create the reality in their own minds. They recognize what is happening, but they intentionally give up what they know to be true. This mode of presence is experienced whenever we watch a movie, view a video, attend a drama, or read a book. For example, when Carlos assigns his learners to watch the movie *Avatar* for his communications course, they may believe events that are happening in the movie which they may never accept in the real world. They may semi-consciously make a decision to put aside their disbelief and accept the premise as being real for the duration of the movie. They may live the actions portrayed in the movie in their minds. No matter what technology or tools we use in our online courses, the important aspect of the experience for the learners is to provide a sense of "being there," a feeling that they are present in the total learning experience.

DIMENSIONS OF THE LEARNER

According to Garrison, Anderson, and Archer (2001), there are three learner dimensions: the interior world, the interface with the real world (perception/ conception process), and the concrete world they share with others. Our interior world is the inner space in which we reflect on, consider, analyze, and synthesize information. We then make a transition through the perceptual/conceptual process to the outer world in which we relate to other people and share our inner feelings and thoughts. Noe (2005) calls this the *enactive perceptual process*. For example, in an online discussion about a specific topic, Amanda reflects on the posted questions, analyzes and synthesizes her thoughts, and comes to a conclusion. She then shares her feelings and thoughts with others in the online learning community.

Throughout the process of using these three dimensions—the interior world, the interface with the real world, and the concrete world—emotions affect thought and then behavior, affecting our experience of presence. Though neglected in the past, the importance of emotions in learning is gaining significance. Emotions are key to the process because they help learners focus their perceptions on particular aspects of a thought and enable them to concentrate on specific situations, connect the affective to the cognitive, and arrive at thoughtful and appropriate decisions (Alcañiz, Bañoa, Botella, & Rey, 2003). Emotions act as a kind of gatekeeper, both with and without the intervention of thought.

According to Salovey and Mayer (1990) and Thorndike and Stein (1937), emotions may be used wisely for positive purposes or for negative manipulation (Weinstein, 1969). Emotional intelligence involves "the ability to perceive accurately, appraise, and express emotion; the ability to access and/or generate feelings when they facilitate thought; the ability to understand emotion and emotional knowledge; and the ability to regulate emotions to promote emotional and intellectual growth" (Salovey & Sluyter, 1997, p. 10).

It is important to note that there are two sides of the emotional coin. One example is a learner who overwhelmingly shares messages that provoke negative emotions in other people and leads the discussion in a negative direction. The other example is a learner who shares ideas related to content concepts and thoughtfully incorporates personal feelings, encouraging others to participate in the discourse in a positive manner. The relatively new area of research in emotional intelligence (Goleman, 1995) tells us that the more we are able to use our emotions in connection with our thought process, the better we are able to clarify our perceptions and make decisions most appropriate to a given situation.

In this research, increased connectivity between thought and emotion is the key to their working together rather than separately (LeDoux, 1996). The Massachusetts Institute of Technology (MIT) is basing its Learning Companion project on the interplay of emotion, thought, and learning. This project is developing an affective companion prototype that will provide emotional support to participants in the learning process, assisting them by helping to alleviate frustration and self-doubt (Picard, Kort, & Reilly, 2004).

If Carlos wants to provide emotional support to learners who are new to his online course, he should include in his orientation materials a detailed explanation of how the online environment can be accessed, how to use the course technology, how to navigate his online course, and how to become active members of the learning community.

THE BEING THERE FOR THE ONLINE LEARNER MODEL

In this chapter we have discussed ways in which presence can be experienced based on the types of experience, modes of presence, and dimensions of the learner. With the types of experience, Carlos can see "how" learning is experienced by his learners. With the modes of presence, he can see "how" the illusion of presence is accomplished. The dimensions of the learner is a three-phase process (inner world, interface with the outer world, and the outer world), through which his learners experience presence.

To synthesize the concepts presented in this chapter and in Chapter 1, we introduce here the Being There for the Online Learner model. It incorporates types of experience, modes of presence, and dimensions of the learner. Online learners interact from within their inner world (interior world) through the perceptual/conceptual process (interface), to the outer world (concrete world).

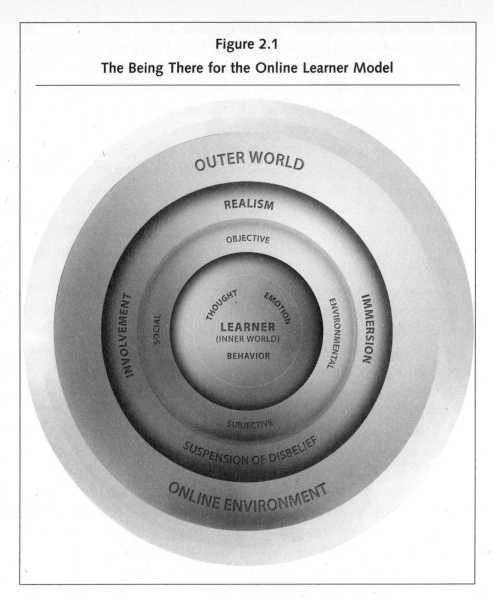

Figure 2.1

The Being There for the Online Learner Model

OUTER WORLD

REALISM

OBJECTIVE

THOUGHT · EMOTION

INVOLVEMENT

SOCIAL

ENVIRONMENTAL

IMMERSION

LEARNER
(INNER WORLD)

BEHAVIOR

SUBJECTIVE

SUSPENSION OF DISBELIEF

ONLINE ENVIRONMENT

Figure 2.1 provides a graphic representation of the model and how these elements interplay.

Understanding the Model

Think of the circular graphic in the figure as a cylinder containing three cylinders inside it, all of them in motion. The dark shaded lines between some of the cylinders highlight the interface between the inner and outer worlds of the learner. The outer cylinder is the physical world of the learner as the learner connects to the online environment via technology. The next two inner cylinders correspond to the types of experience and modes of presence. These two inner cylinders blend into each other and occur in combination with each other. Think of the center cylinder as the learner and the learner's perceptual process, which includes the dynamic interplay between thought, emotion, and behavior.

Throughout the process, emotions affect thought and then behavior, affecting the experience of presence in the online environment. These types of experience may be subjective, objective, social, or environmental or a combination of more than one. As we have seen, in the online environment learners can experience presence through realism, immersion, involvement, and suspension of disbelief. If instructors keep this model in mind, they can become aware of and understand what is necessary to make online presence happen.

Putting the Model to Work

How can Carlos envision his online course with a sense of presence? By following the model, he places his learners at the center of his teaching. He knows that his learners bring thoughts, emotions, and behaviors to the learning experience as a result of their perceptual process. This process includes their inner world, interface with the outer (concrete) world, and the outer (concrete) world. The entire process takes place in the online environment. The design of an online course should take into consideration the four types of experience—subjective, objective, social, and environmental—that affect participant learning depending on the content being taught, and the ways—realism, immersion, involvement, and suspension of disbelief—in which learners experience a sense of presence in the online course. Carlos and his learners experience a sense of presence by thinking, feeling, and behaving through interactions. The result is "being there" and "being together" for the online learning experience.

Amanda was anxious when she received the information packet for her online course. She felt overwhelmed and had many questions. Her feelings indicated that she did not understand the types of experience that are possible in the online learning environment. She did not know what to expect, and as a result, her emotions drove her perceptions. Novice learners often feel overwhelmed in this way because they do not understand the online environment. However, a well-designed course that clearly explains and implements the types of experience and modes of presence can alleviate this tension.

Similarly, Carlos's feelings of insecurity stemmed from his lack of knowledge about the online environment. His misconceptions overshadowed his ability to be self-confident about his new venture as an online instructor. He had not begun to design his online course and was feeling anxious. His anxiety focused his attention on the need to become aware of and understand the online environment. Understanding the types of experiences that can create presence, the modes of presence in which his learners can experience presence through his teachings, and the dimensions of the learner can help Carlos become aware of the concept of presence.

SUMMARY

The sense of presence is clearly part of a psychological and emotional process and, therefore, is a state of mind. The concept of presence is relative, and for the novice learner it should be dealt with before the online course starts. For the inexperienced instructor, creating presence should be addressed in training and included in the preparation for designing the first online courses. Designing an online course that creates a sense of presence involves more than merely moving a face-to-face course to the online environment. The course must be rethought and the materials and activities adapted to create a sense of presence. In Chapter 3, we will provide an instructional design framework based on the Being There for the Online Learner model. The framework uses the determinants of presence as design components to create the online learning experience.

Designing Your Online Course with a Sense of Presence

Scenario 1. Amanda has gone through the online orientation packet for her online course. As she reads it, she becomes more excited about her decision to take the course. Her instructor's letter makes her feel welcome. The other materials are so well organized that she feels she knows what she is getting into. Her instructor gives her access to the online course and provides all the information that she had questions about. Now she knows what the online course will look like (its focus and format), what strategies she will be involved with and how she will be able to meet her classmates, the role that her instructor will play, what technologies will be used in the course, and who to call for support. She is beginning to feel more confident that she made the right decision in enrolling for the course.

Scenario 2. After attending the training session on how to move his face-to-face course to the online environment, Carlos redesigned his existing course with an awareness of the importance of creating a sense of presence, considering the determinants of presence. Based on his focus and content, he decided to use a group-based format that included the same interactive strategies he uses in his face-to-face course. However, he adapted them for the online environment and uploaded them to the learning management system. He created a course orientation, activated his course in the learning management system, and sent a welcome letter and orientation materials to his twenty-five learners two weeks prior to the start of the course.

Although his role as an instructor continues to be the same as in his face-to-face course, he now intentionally considers his role from an online perspective so that he can create a sense of presence. He has also become aware of the importance of instructional and technical support, making the technology transparent and the learners the center of the design process.

Designing your online course with a sense of presence requires understanding the multifaceted concept of presence. In order for presence to be integrated into the design of your online course, you must understand the perceptual nature of the learner. In Chapter 2, we described the perceptual nature of the learner and presented a model for understanding the concept of presence. In this chapter we will offer an instructional design framework, based on the Being There for the Online Learner model. This framework uses the determinants of presence as design components to create the online learning experience. We will provide three examples of online courses to illustrate how to use the framework to create a sense of presence. In addition, we will provide an overview of how to prepare yourself as an online instructor and get your learners "there" for your online course. It is beyond the scope of this book to focus on the design aspects of online teaching and learning, but we will direct you to training and design resources.

DETERMINANTS OF PRESENCE

The determinants of presence are the components of the design process that guide the creation of a sense of presence in the online environment. These components are the type and focus of the content, the format of the learning experience, the interactive strategies implemented, the role played by the instructor, the type of technology used in the course, and the kinds of support provided.

Type and Focus of Content

The type and focus of content can influence the way in which a sense of presence is created in an online course. Course disciplines have a decided effect on the design of the instructional materials, the management and execution of the instruction, and the relationship of the learners with the instructor and each other (Lehman, 1977, 1991; Munro, 1998; Olgren, 1993). The type and focus of content also depend on the mindset of the instructor and the course objectives to be achieved.

Some courses focus more on process than content. For example, an online instructional design course may focus on creating instruction for adult learners involving five design phases. In contrast, an online communications course may focus on intercultural issues involving several countries. The two courses require different ways of creating presence. The online instructional design course might involve learners in completing tasks in small groups (that is, it might have a process focus). The online communications course might engage learners through discussion to debate controversial intercultural issues occurring in different countries (that is, have a content focus).

Format of the Learning Experience

The format of the learning experience can vary from individual self-paced to group-based or a mix of both. In self-paced courses, learners are self-directed, have flexibility in doing the assignments and completing the course, can access the course at their own pace and time, and can communicate with the instructor or tutor on an as-needed basis for feedback and clarification of course assignments. In this format, presence can be created through video, audio, and direct communication via telephone, e-mail, and other methods. In the case of group-based courses, like Carlos's course, learners interact with him and each other. The course design intentionally focuses on the group collaboration or cooperation through discussions, projects, and fieldwork. In a mixed format, a blend of self-paced and group-based is specifically designed to provide both individual and group learning experiences.

Interactive Strategies

Interactive strategies are approaches used to engage learners with you, with the content, and with other learners. They can take the form of personalizing, discussions, case studies, role-plays, team projects, scavenger hunts, debates, interviews, guest experts for questions and answers, and many more. These interactive strategies (or activities) will be explained in detail in Chapter 4.

The Role of the Instructor

The role of the instructor in online environments has evolved from one of a source of authority to one of support in the teaching-learning process. In this new role, instructors become instructional designers who design the online experience for learners, facilitators who engage the learner in the learning process, catalysts who instigate conversations, and also learners themselves who partici-pate in the learning process (Conceição-Runlee, 2001).

As the instructional designer creating your course, it is important to begin developing the course ahead of time using a timeline to ensure that all the course components are completed before the course starts. If you are designing the course by yourself, you need to be sure to avoid working on the course design at the last minute; however, remember to remain creative and spontaneous when the occasion calls for it. If you are working with a team (that is, graphic designer, instructional designer, technology specialist, and so on), make sure that roles and tasks are clearly defined, there is direct communication with your team, and the timeline is followed.

As a facilitator, you may want to assign leadership roles to learners and par-ticipate from the sidelines without losing your instructor presence. During dis-cussions, allow learners to share insights and lead conversations while you participate simply by clarifying issues. As a catalyst, your role is to challenge learners' thinking through questions and discussion. These two roles are often performed together.

Other roles that you may take in the online environment include supporter, mentor, tutor, observer, and evaluator. As a supporter, you can assist learners with special needs. As a mentor, you can guide learners in ways to succeed in the online course by meeting one-on-one. As a tutor, you can help learners who are working independently with you. As an observer, you can stay in the back-ground, watching your learners and intervening when necessary. As an evaluator, you can provide feedback throughout the online course by assessing learners' performance.

In all of these instructor roles, you may also be a learner. Here, teaching no longer takes the form of one-way instruction with the instructor at the center transmitting information. Rather, knowledge becomes a shared activity of the online learning community, part of a collective effort between you and your learners (Conceição-Runlee, 2001).

It is evident that Carlos takes on multiple roles—designer, lecturer, facilitator, and evaluator—when he teaches his face-to-face courses. Moving and adapting his courses to the online environment involved rethinking his role as an instruc-tor so that he could create a sense of presence.

Type of Technology

When you consider which type of technology to use in your course, keep in mind that it should become transparent. This means it should not be the course focus or a learning distraction; rather, it should be user-friendly. Learners should be able to interface with the technology as if they were taking a face-to-face class. When selecting the technology for your course, consider the number of course participants and the potential and limitations of the specific technology. Also, as the instructor, you should be comfortable with the technology.

Often online courses are designed with asynchronous interactions, which provide flexibility with place, time, and pace. However, in an asynchronous format you may miss the real-time interaction with the learners. To compensate, you may want to blend synchronous technologies with your online courses. If you do this, you will need to take time zones into consideration and offer these real-time sessions more than once, in different time slots.

If you have access to technologies or software programs other than the learning management system (LMS), you may want to consider using sounds and video that can enhance the learning experience and create a sense of presence. Sounds can be brought in through the use of instructor voice on podcast or simple audio recordings of lectures. Videos can provide lab demonstrations and illustrations of case examples. For learners with hearing needs, captioning audio may be crucial. For learners with visual needs, texts and images will need to be modified. If using sophisticated technology is beyond your skills and time, it will be helpful to seek the technology support center in your organization.

For an inexperienced online instructor like Carlos, inserting new technologies into an online course should be a developmental process. He may want to consider adding complex technologies slowly and only add new technologies that meet his course objectives.

Kinds of Support Provided

Online courses cannot function without instructional and technical support. Support can eliminate many of the potential barriers that could reduce the sense of presence. Instructional support provides learners with psychological and emotional assistance throughout the online course. Technical support is also critical throughout the course to assist both you and your learners in creating and maintaining presence without distraction. With adequate technical support, problems are diminished and technology becomes transparent. There is no doubt that Amanda needed instructional and technical support when she embarked on her new learning venture. With so many questions, she could well have been a candidate for dropping out before the course even started.

Now, imagine that you have designed your online course with a sense of presence and feel confident that everything will work well. Support is one of the keys to making this happen. Often instructors disregard the importance of support. Instructional and technical support puts the technology in the background and brings the learners to the forefront. We will cover instructional and technical support in more detail in Chapter 4.

FRAMEWORK FOR DESIGNING ONLINE COURSES WITH A SENSE OF PRESENCE

In this chapter, we propose an instructional design framework that uses the Being There for the Online Learner model as a foundation for understanding presence and the determinants of presence as the design components for creating a sense of presence in the online environment. The sense of presence should be intentionally incorporated into the design of the course during the preplanning phase using the determinants of presence. If you teach a predesigned course, it is still important that you are familiar with what makes presence happen. Figure 3.1 depicts the framework for designing online courses with a sense of presence.

Understanding the Framework

Looking at the framework, you see the Being There for the Online Learner model on the left; it helps you become aware of and understand what is necessary to make presence happen online. The arrow running from the model to the instructor represents the instructor's awareness of how presence occurs online. The arrow from the instructor to the determinants of presence represents the path the instructor takes to design the course with a sense of presence. The determinants of presence are the components of the design process that guide the instructor's creation of presence in the online environment. The arrows from the determinants of presence to the model and from the model to the determinants of presence show the continuous action involved in using and revisiting the components of the framework.

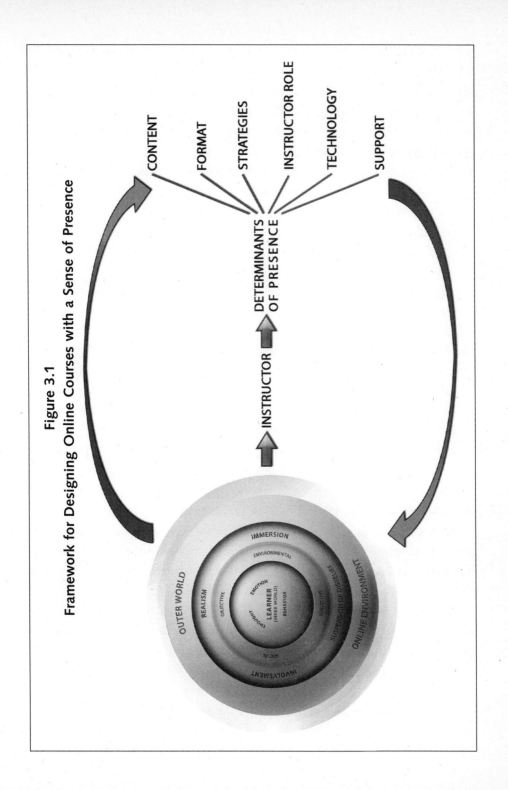

Figure 3.1
Framework for Designing Online Courses with a Sense of Presence

Using the Framework

Because online presence is an elusive, complex concept, using a systematic approach to it can guide you in your course design process. Our design framework can help you identify the multifaceted components of an online course, carefully plan and design prior to the delivery of the course, and manage the instructional process to ensure effective learning outcomes. We will provide three examples of online courses that utilize the framework. Each will be explained in detail indicating how the determinants of presence, types of experience, and modes of presence may be used by the instructor to create a sense of presence online. Table 3.1 provides an outline of the three online courses and the determinants of presence.

History of Philosophy Course   This self-paced philosophy course looks at the reappearance of recurrent problems in the history of intellectual thought. The course focuses on the historical development of the Western philosophical tradition, from pre-Socratics to contemporary thinkers. The course is available for learners for sixteen weeks with six units lasting three to four weeks each. Learners complete the units at their own pace. The instructor is available at specific times for electronic office hours. It is the learners' responsibility and choice to be in contact with the instructor during the electronic office hours.

Learners are required to complete unit readings, review instructor videos about the different philosophical thinkers, complete course quizzes, conduct interviews with the instructor, and critically assess the recurrent problems presented by the instructor through videos. In this case, the instructor role is one of course designer, facilitator, and tutor. Instructor video and interviews are important presence elements of the course. Videos are located in the learning management system, and biweekly interactions between instructor and learner are conducted via e-mail or Web-based videoconferencing.

Communication and feedback create personal and interactive involvement between the learner and instructor, giving the learner the illusion of "being there" with the instructor (subjective and social experience). When learners are actively involved in dynamic conversations with the instructor through e-mail and Web-based videoconferencing (involvement), their interactions become lively and provide a sense of being together in the same room (realism).

Table 3.1

Examples of Determinants of Presence for Three Online Courses

CONTENT TYPE AND FOCUS	LEARNING EXPERIENCE FORMAT	INTERACTIVE STRATEGIES	INSTRUCTOR ROLE	TYPE OF TECHNOLOGY THAT ENABLES PRESENCE	SUPPORT
History of Philosophy: content focus	Self-paced	Interview, instructor video	Designer, facilitator, tutor	LMS, e-mail, videoconferencing	Instructional, technical
Creative Writing: content and process focus	Group-based	Group discussion, team project, instructor demonstration	Designer, facilitator, catalyst, mentor	LMS, discussion board, video illustrations	Instructional, technical
Technical Project Management: process focus	Group-based	Team problem solving, group discussion	Designer, catalyst, observer, evaluator	Discussion board, Web conferencing, mobile devices	Instructional, technical

Creative Writing Course   This creative writing course focuses on experimental narrative through poems and stories, including image and text relationships, to examine how media and narrative actively construct meaning. Learners are required to work both independently and in a group. Independent assignments include creating poems or stories. Learners view video pictures presented by the instructor with no descriptions. They then translate these video pictures into narratives and share them with the instructor and the rest of the class. On the discussion board, they critique and comment on one another's work based on creativity, similarities and differences in interpretation, and ways in which picture interpretations could be grouped into story themes.

In small groups, based on the story themes of the video pictures, the learners create and refine a group story. Group stories are produced as an online book using a PDF file or hypertext formats. Group collaboration to produce the online book is accomplished via the discussion board and Web conferencing. As a final assignment, all learners use the online discussion board to talk about the relationship between image and text to examine how media and narrative actively construct meaning. During the entire course, the instructor works with learners to facilitate and mentor the process, clarify procedures, and challenge group thinking.

The course incorporates these activities in order to create a sense of presence: instructor video illustration of the work of art (subjective experience), individual sharing and group critiquing (social experience), team project (social and environmental experience), and group discussion (social experience). The instructor video illustration is a realistic representation of a contemporary work of art (realism). However, while viewing the work of art, the learners create its reality in their own minds by allowing themselves to suspend their own analytical faculties, and accepting this premise as being real (suspension of disbelief). This is a semi-conscious decision in which they put aside their disbelief and create their own interpretation of the work of art. They then share their interpretation in an open forum and critique and comment on each other's interpretations (group involvement).

Through the creation and posting of the video illustration, the instructor gives the learners a sense of being personally and psychologically in the same space (subjective experience). The video begins with the instructor's introduction of the assignment. In a conversational manner, the instructor shows the work of art and explains the task to be accomplished. Then, learners are involved in "show and tell" and share through an online conversation in the discussion board their interpretations of the work of art (social experience).

The team project engages the learners in collaborative work that at times becomes so lively that they feel they are together in the same space (objective experience). For the final discussion, the learners and instructor engage in interactive conversations, sharing their feelings and thoughts about the meaning of the relationship between the work of art and the narratives they create (social experience). This activity involves complex thinking and emotional engagement, resulting in a sense of team presence and team ownership.

Technical Project Management Course This technical project management course focuses on strategies, tools, and methods to plan, schedule, budget, and execute electrical engineering projects. It simulates the real-world experience in which learners become immersed in a team project experience. In this process-based course, learners apply methods and tools to enhance organizational and management skills. This course also helps them learn how to use specific management software and mobile devices. It attracts participants from around the world who are working professionals and uses asynchronous and synchronous online communication strategies as well as mobile devices.

This course is located in a learning management system and also utilizes Web conferencing and handheld devices. Participants learn about working in teams. They are divided into small teams, assigned team roles, and work collaboratively on a real-world project throughout the course. In the learning management system, learners complete and present team tasks asynchronously, sharing their project progress with the whole class in an open forum (social experience). On a biweekly basis, the teams schedule two Web conferencing meetings (to accommodate the various time zones) in which they brainstorm and discuss team project tasks. Using their handheld devices, team members can access portions of the online course for study, collect field data for the team project, and share new information with team members (social and environmental experience).

The instructor designs the course; serves as a catalyst to assist learners in creating, developing, and implementing the team project; observes the team progress; and assesses the team process. During the course, the instructor provides detailed feedback on presented tasks for each team and conducts a mid-course survey (environmental experience), in which participants are asked to provide anonymous feedback on the course through critical incidents (see Chapter 4 for sample critical incident questions). At the end of the course, the learners complete a final course evaluation containing questions related to the course design, content, and teaching. The instructor is available for electronic office hours twice a week and serves as a consultant on the team project management (social experience).

Presence is facilitated through the use of various technologies and team projects. Technology in this context becomes transparent; it is merely there to facilitate the interactions and communications among learners and instructor. Team tasks require group involvement for the creation of the team project through fieldwork, brainstorming, and sharing. All learners use the online open forum for presenting team project progress and commenting on each other's projects (involvement). Instructor presence is accessible through electronic office hours and team task feedback. The mid-course survey allows the instructor to check in on learners' perceptions about the course and get a sense of their feelings of presence. The course uses immersion to create presence by involving participants in a simulated experience of the real world (realism and immersion). Illusion is created for learners as they work on a common project virtually that can be applied in the real world. During this process, learners must imagine that they are meeting in a real office, presenting and discussing information with each other in the same room, and working from the same documents and materials.

Making Presence Happen in Your Online Course

With this framework in mind, you can use the determinants of presence to design presence in your online course by considering the types of experience and modes of presence that influence learning and meet course outcomes. The three online course examples just described showed how the determinants of presence may be used to create a sense of presence in a variety of courses. The manner in which it can be accomplished depends on the course discipline, the format of the learning experience, the interactive strategies used to engage learners, the personality and skills of the instructor, the types of technology selected, and the instructional and technical support provided. The design process is not a linear one; rather it is one of continuous action in which the instructor uses and revisits the components of the framework.

GETTING YOURSELF "THERE" FOR YOUR ONLINE COURSE

Your training as an online instructor must begin with an understanding of the differences between face-to-face and online teaching. Instructional and technical support are key to your success in this new environment, as is the support of your organization. Developing an online course can be a challenge for both novices and seasoned online instructors. After training, you will be better prepared to teach online and understand what presence means in the online environment, be able to create and incorporate presence into your online course, and be ready to deliver your course.

Training

Remember how, at the beginning of this chapter, Carlos redesigned his existing course after attending a training session? If you are new to online teaching like Carlos, you should begin with training. This includes becoming familiar with the learning management system, its features, and its limitations. You can take scheduled training sessions or workshops or work closely with an instructional designer who has learning management system expertise. Or you might team up with experienced colleagues who have created online courses that have proven to be effective. If your organization does not offer design support, look into the training resources provided in Appendix 1.

Whatever method of training you choose, it is essential that you be prepared for what needs to be accomplished before, during, and at the end of your online course by adapting the course materials and considering learners' needs.

Creating Your Online Course

After you have become familiar with and confident about the learning management system software, the next step is to identify an existing course that you plan to move to the online environment and start the design process. Table 3.2 provides a sample course design task and timeline for an existing course that is moving to the online environment.

Although it is outside the scope of this book to provide detailed instructions on designing a new online course or moving an existing course from the face-to-face to the online environment, you can find a list of resources for designing online courses in Appendix 2.

Table 3.2
Course Design Task and Timeline for an Existing Course

TASK	TIMELINE
Identify course to be taught.	4 to 12 weeks before course starts
Review course content and divide content into units.	
Develop course objectives, outcomes, and assessments.	
Create a course outline (content, activities, and timeline).	
Decide on the course format.	
Develop interactive strategies.	
Identify the role you will play as instructor.	
Select additional technology for your course.	
Ensure instructional and technical support.	
Create your course syllabus to match the online environment.	
Consider the types of experience you would like your learners to have.	
Determine the ways (modes) in which you would like you and your learners to experience a sense of presence.	
Decide which features you plan to use in the learning management system and set them up.	
Create and insert content materials and activities using audio, video, and text files.	
Develop course orientation materials.	3 to 6 weeks before course starts
Activate the course in the learning management system.	2 weeks before course starts
Send out the course welcome letter.	2 weeks before course starts

Incorporating a Sense of Presence in Your Online Course

Table 3.3 illustrates ways in which you can incorporate a sense of presence into your online course. By identifying the types of activity, interaction, and presence, you can determine where presence can be integrated throughout the teaching process (before, during, and end of course). Table 3.3 is not all-inclusive. Types

Table 3.3

Incorporating a Sense of Presence in the Online Course

	TYPE OF ACTIVITY	TYPE OF INTERACTION	TYPE OF PRESENCE
Before the course	Welcome letter	Instructor-learners	Objective/subjective
	Orientation	Learner-learner	Social and environmental
	Scavenger hunt	Learner-instructor	Objective/subjective
	Introductions		
	Logistics		
	Self-assessment		
	Learning styles		
	Electronic office hours		
During the course	Announcements	Instructor-learners	Objective/subjective
	Feedback	Instructor-learners	Objective
	Videos,	All	Subjective
	Real-time Web conferencing	All	Social
	Team projects	Learner-learner	Social/objective
	Logistics	All	Objective/subjective
	Simulations	All	Subjective
	Case studies	All	Objective/subjective
	Electronic office hours	Learner-instructor	Objective/subjective
End of course	Announcements	Learner-instructor	Objective/subjective
	Feedback	Learner-instructor	Objective
	Final project presentations	Learner-instructor-learner	Social
	Course evaluation	Learner-instructor	Objective
	Electronic office hours	Learner-instructor	Objective/subjective

of interactions or presence may vary depending on the discipline. Our intention here is to stimulate your thinking on the types of interaction and presence you may include in your online course. More details about the activities mentioned in the table will be given in Chapter 4.

GETTING YOUR LEARNERS "THERE" FOR YOUR ONLINE COURSE

Learners come to online courses with different experiences and expectations. You must be prepared to accommodate learners with a wide range of needs. These learners may be totally new to learning with technology, like Amanda, or be seasoned online learners. No matter who your learners are, you must provide services to meet their needs.

Before your course starts, be sure to provide a detailed orientation for your learners. The orientation serves as an entry point to your course. Send a welcome letter to them. This welcome letter may be the first contact they have with you and can set the tone for the entire course. Often a welcome letter is mailed or e-mailed at least two weeks prior to the start of the course. It should introduce you to your learners, provide information about your course, and invite them to participate in the course orientation. A sample welcome letter will be provided in Chapter 4.

The course orientation may take the form of a scavenger hunt, in which participants complete activities. A typical online course orientation welcomes learners to the course; explains how to navigate that specific course; gives details about course expectations; provides guidelines for setting time to work on the course; explains how to contact the instructor; informs learners about participation expectations; and provides Netiquette rules. A sample scavenger hunt will be described in Chapter 4.

Online course orientation activities not only set the tone for the entire course but also create an opportunity for learners to get ready for a safe and comfortable environment, as in the case of Amanda. You may want to use the first week of the course for relationship-building through "getting-to-know-each-other" forums where all class members participate in introducing themselves and sharing personal anecdotes. It is also common to divide learners into small groups and involve them in logistical tasks to set group guidelines, determine leadership roles, and identify expected timelines. These activities are all critical in creating a sense of instructor and learner presence. Learners who miss the first week of orientation activities are less likely to maintain the same level of participation and motivation and tend to fall behind on assignments and activities. A well-designed precourse orientation can help learners feel they are part of the learning community and are "there" and "together" from the beginning of the course.

In the beginning of this chapter, we saw that Amanda's confidence in taking the online course has increased. Her fears of the unknown are disappearing. She now understands the structure of the online course and course expectations. This feeling of confidence comes in part thanks to the well-designed welcome letter and orientation materials that she received from her instructor, which make her feel that she is already part of the online course even though it has not yet formally begun.

Carlos is gaining confidence about his online course, too. He developed it using the framework that includes the determinants of presence and uploaded his course materials to the learning management system. He sent out his welcome letter and orientation materials and is now ready for the course to begin. Taking a systematic approach in creating presence guided Carlos in the design process. The framework helped him identify the components of his online course, thoroughly plan and design prior to the delivery of the course, and will facilitate the management of the instructional process throughout his online course.

SUMMARY

In this chapter we incorporated the Being There for the Online Learner model in an instructional design framework for creating online learning with a sense of presence. The model places the learner at the center of the learning experience. Our framework uses the determinants of presence as the design components for creating online instruction. The Being There for the Online Learner model serves as a foundation for understanding the sense of presence. In our framework the sense of presence should be intentionally integrated into the online course during the preplanning phase. In Chapter 4, we will describe activities that can create and enhance a sense of presence throughout the online course.

Activities That Create a Sense of Presence in Your Online Course

Scenario 1. Once Amanda became aware of how important it was to be involved in the online environment through activities and interaction, her understanding of a sense of presence gave her a social, psychological, and emotional perspective on being an online learner. She soon became an active member of the online community, engaging with her instructor and classmates in the group discussions and team project. Now she feels a part of the community. As she progressed through the first portion of the course, she began to take leadership roles by volunteering to be a small-group facilitator. She also helped others with tips on how to overcome online feelings of isolation, frustration, and dissatisfaction in the "Share 'Almost' Anything" open forum. Through her help, these feelings were replaced with a sense of trust and relationship building. It looks like she has taken ownership of her learning, the technology has become more transparent for her, and her sense of presence in the online learning experience is "there" both individually and with her classmates.

Scenario 2. As Carlos progressed in teaching his first online course, he realized that being "there" for the online learners required a different mindset. In his face-to-face courses, his instructional presentations were in the form of lectures and he could easily see how his learners were responding to his teaching. He felt he was socially, psychologically, and emotionally with them. He was able to see his learners during their small-group work. In his online course, he is still using lecture-based strategies, but now he is recording them and uploading them to the learning management system. However, where his live lectures in the face-to-face environment gave him a sense of presence with his learners, he now feels abandoned because he pre-records his lectures. He also feels ignored because when he posts messages no one comments directly to him. He has come to realize that, by checking his learners' access through the LMS progress report, he can see that they are communicating directly with each other and actively accessing and participating in the different course areas. He realizes that although his instructor role is similar to his role in face-to-face courses, his strategies must be different. In order for his learners to feel that he is "there," he sends out biweekly video announcements using social networking tools, is available for electronic office hours weekly via Skype, participates in the general and small-group discussions, and provides individual feedback to his learners when necessary.

Designing an online course with a sense of presence is an important part of the online teaching experience, but it is not everything. As the instructor, you should also think, feel, and behave with a sense of presence once you are in the online environment. The same applies to the learners. They too need to be involved in the dynamic interplay that results from interactions with others, guided by their emotions, which direct both thought and behavior. Each individual needs to make presence happen. The sense of presence can be enhanced if you incorporate activities that will help your learners feel they are "there" and "together" with others.

This chapter will describe activities that can create a sense of presence in your online course. We offer these activities using the determinants of presence, which are part of the framework for designing online courses with a sense of presence. These activities are based on their potential sequence: before the course begins, during the course, and at the end of the course. We will describe the types of activities to include in each sequence. Finally, we will offer approaches and questions for gathering information to help you determine if you have created presence in your online course. It is important to keep in mind the Being There for the Online Learner model when incorporating the activities described in this chapter. The model places the learner at the center of the design process and considers the types of experiences and modes of presence you may want to include.

BEFORE THE COURSE BEGINS

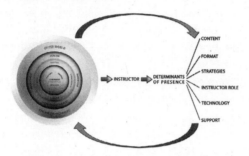

Determinants of Presence

Based on the framework for designing online courses with a sense of presence, it is important for you to consider how to use the determinants of presence to design experiences that create presence before the course begins.

Table 4.1 describes how to use the determinants of presence to design an online course.

Course Activities

As mentioned in Chapter 3, precourse orientation and activities set the tone for the entire online course. At this time you can obtain information about your learners' backgrounds and interests and share information about yourself with them. It provides an opportunity for you to connect and start creating a sense of presence with the group. It is best to implement these orientation activities before and through the first week of the online course.

Welcome Letter To introduce yourself to your learners, provide information about the course, and invite them to participate in the course orientation, we suggest that you send a course welcome letter. Recall that the welcome letter that Amanda received in her packet of materials made her aware of the different aspects of the online experience and gave her a sense of confidence. You may

Table 4.1

Determinants of Presence: Before the Online Course Begins

DETERMINANTS	DESCRIPTION
Content	Your content for precourse activities should focus on how to get acquainted with the technology and course participants.
Format	The format of your activities should include a mix of self-paced and group-based. For example, the course orientation tasks should be completed by the participants at their own pace and in their own time. Some of these tasks should involve group activities.
Strategies	Through online discussion forums, you and your learners can engage in conversations to get to know each other.
Role of instructor	At this point, you take the role of a facilitator by guiding learners, clarifying issues, and encouraging participation.
Technology	Learners participate in the course orientation tasks through the learning management system, but you may also consider other technologies (such as audio or video announcements) to introduce yourself and enhance your presence in the course.
Support	Technical support is especially important at the beginning of the course. If learners are not able to easily access and navigate the technology, they are likely to drop out. Technical support can be provided through you as the instructor, or learners can be directed to a help desk in your organization.

want to send your welcome letter with information about the course, the required textbooks, and instructions on getting started. The letter should be written in a personal and conversational manner to help learners begin to feel a sense of presence in your online course. Exhibit 4.1 provides a sample course welcome letter. You will see that this sample letter in an adult education course introduces the instructor to the course participants, explains the course expectations, encourages learners to participate in the course orientation, and sets a stimulating and exciting tone that will foster enthusiasm for the course.

Scavenger Hunt The course orientation activities may take the form of a scavenger hunt that guides your learners to discover and learn about the course. The

Exhibit 4.1
Sample Online Course Welcome Letter

Hello everyone,

Welcome to the online course [course name and number]! I am your instructor for this course and I am looking forward to working with you. The purpose of this course is to [course purpose]. You may want to purchase the following course textbook(s) [textbook authors and title] as soon as you get this message.

This course will provide an opportunity for you to participate in individual and interactive activities. My courses often involve the work of teams. This one is no exception. I have already set up the teams for the course. You should be able to log into the learning management system and search for your name on the team areas. I tried to place people in teams with individuals they have not worked with in courses I have taught. Teams will remain the same for the entire course, but the team areas will be open for anyone to view the progress of the discussion and team projects.

I strongly encourage you to read the orientation materials. The orientation materials provide important information for the first week of the course, a critical part of the course to set the tone for the rest of the semester. One area I would like you to pay close attention to is how messages should be posted in the group area in the learning management system. For the team project, team members may choose how they want to organize the messages.

This course is always stimulating to teach because of the creative nature of the assignments. We should all have fun this semester. The skills you will gain from participating in this course can be powerful for your future as an educator and trainer. So take this opportunity to embrace in a challenging, creative, and exciting venture.

See you online!
Your Instructor

scavenger hunt can incorporate tips on how to navigate through your course, how to participate in the course interactions, and how to gain confidence in the online environment. Activities for the scavenger hunt might include tasks that teach how to navigate the learning management system, ask students to complete an individual data sheet and the Getting-to-Know-You Survey, provide introductory interactions with the instructor and other learners, and offer a review of course expectations. While delineating the structure of your course, your instructions should take a personal tone, as though you were talking with your learners. Exhibit 4.2 provides a sample course scavenger hunt. Learners carry out these tasks both before and during the course.

Exhibit 4.2
Sample Course Scavenger Hunt

Welcome to Course [Course Name and Number]!

Taking an online course can be very exciting and satisfying, but it can also be frustrating and discouraging. You will find that the online learning environment allows you to attend class whenever you wish, day or night, seven days a week. Each time you "connect" with the class you will find that others have responded to your comments and brought up new perspectives on topics that you have not thought about. The online environment will allow you to synthesize the readings and activities you are involved with while you reflect upon their application on your personal and professional life.

Learning online presents its own rewards and challenges. Due to its unusual availability, you may find that learning online does not easily fit in your schedule as a regular class might, because you are responsible for setting your own time to work on the course. You may also discover that it can become difficult to carry on several conversations simultaneously or that you have difficulty processing all of the information you receive. And it may be disconcerting to express your opinions in text form only, without having a clear mental picture of who is "listening." Also, you may have difficulty navigating the structure, asking questions, and submitting your assignments. The following activities will provide tips on how to overcome these challenges.

The first week of class is very important for everyone to get to know each other and get ready for a safe and comfortable group discussion throughout the course.

Complete the Following Tasks before the First Week of the Course:

NEW TO THE ONLINE ENVIRONMENT: If you have never taken an online course, I strongly encourage you to start with the learning management system instructions document. [Your organization should have this document available to learners.]

WELCOME ANNOUNCEMENT: When you first log into the course you will see my welcome announcement. Please watch this video. Note that announcements will be posted in this area throughout the course on a weekly basis.

- *Explore the learning management system course website:* Be sure to visit all areas of the site: Announcements, Content, Discussions, Links, Drop Box, Grades, e-mail, Classlist, Chat, etc. It is important that you know your way around the course environment!

- *Check the course content:* Select Content on the top menu. Under course information, open the course syllabus, readings, and outline and browse through them. You may want to print them out for your records.

- *Course orientation:* Now browse through the Course Orientation section. Explore the links and files listed under this section.

- *Electronic reserve:* Find the link for the Electronic Reserve (e-Reserve) area at our University. (Hint: Look in the Top Menu again for "Links.") To access e-Reserve, use your university login and password.

- *Introduce yourself:* Introduce yourself to the class: select Discussions on the top menu, select the General Discussion Area, and then select "Introducing Yourself." Share information about your job, family, or hobbies that you would like your classmates to know about. You may include a picture of yourself. To post your personal introduction just click on the

Continued

"Add message" button on the right side of the screen as soon as you enter the forum. Write your message and then select the "Submit" button.

INDIVIDUAL DATA SHEET: Download the file "Individual Data Sheet" from the *Course Orientation* area. Complete the Individual Data Sheet and upload to the folder *Individual Data* Sheet in the Drop Box.

GETTING-TO-KNOW-YOU SURVEY: In the Course Orientation area select "Getting-to-Know-You Survey," complete the survey, and then submit it.

Complete the Following Tasks by the End of the First Week of the Course:

GET TO KNOW YOUR TEAM: Look for the team area that contains your name. Under your team area, select Logistics, and then start communicating with your team members. The first thing you will want to do is get to know your team members. You will be working with the same team during the whole course. It has been common for learners to come up with a name that represents the team characteristics. If you decide on a team name, please e-mail it to me.

SCHEDULE THE MEMBER ROLES FOR ONLINE DISCUSSIONS: Complete the chart for assigning discussion roles for each unit and post it in the learning management system in the Team Tasks Area. Use the template posted in the Course Orientation area. Save the file with the name of your team.

START READINGS: Start readings ahead of time, so you do not fall behind during the course. This course will involve a lot of tasks based on the read-ings. Unit 1 readings are available in the Content area of the learning management system.

For the Rest of the Course:

SET ASIDE TIME TO WORK ON THE COURSE: You must allow a regular time and space for working on this course. This course has been designed so that it will take about the same amount of participation time as you would spend in a normal three-credit classroom course. The benefit of an online course is its flexibility (you can work on it whenever and from wherever you have access to the Internet). But flexibility can also be a trap. So, plan on spending between two and three hours "logged on" every week, just as you would spend time in class. In addition, find time to do the readings and assignments.

The online discussions will be more enjoyable if you spend that time during three or four sittings during the week. Some learners find it helpful to log on every day, or at least five to six days a week, and therefore to work on the course in smaller amounts of time. By checking in almost every day you'll know if something new has been posted, you'll be able to keep up with the discussion threads, and you will not fall behind with your readings and assignments. This will allow you to post your opinions and get feedback on ideas, rather than just reading after the fact what everyone else has said. In other words, this online course will be more interactive to the extent you frequently read and contribute.

ASK QUESTIONS: Don't be afraid to let me know if you can't make something work, don't know how to do something, or don't understand. Send me an e-mail message or call me at 800-[mynumber]. The best way to reach me is via e-mail because I frequently check it.

PARTICIPATE: Whether you are working alone or on a group/team project, contribute your ideas, perspectives, and comments on the subject. Be sure to read the comments of your classmates—they may do the same job you do and can offer valuable insights and resources. It is a good idea to make at least one contribution each time you are online. Part of your course grade will be based on your active, thoughtful messages in the computer conference. You should plan to make at least three thoughtful and reflective contributions to the discussion per week. Length is not particularly desired for each posting; more important is its benefit to the discussion, the richness of the ideas, and the extent to which it "weaves" into what others have been saying.

READ OTHERS' NOTES: You may consider reading all of the "unread" messages before making your own comment; if not, you will not know whether someone has already made your point. You should be concerned with keeping track of the specific posting to which you wanted to respond. So while you are reading, keep track of the message and general ideas you want to state. Try to determine what has not been said yet that you feel is important, or what experience you bring to this topic or task that other

Continued

course members may not have. Try to add a synthesis or additional analytical comment advancing the discussion to a deeper level of consideration. Refer to the literature (readings) as much as you can.

KEEP TRACK OF THE THREADS: Discussion "threads" are sometimes hard to follow, especially if your comments or others' comments do not immediately follow the posting they reference. Always reference the comment you are responding to. This will allow you and others to go back and use the message thread feature of the learning management system to review a set of replies on one topic.

CHECK THE FORUM LOCATION BEFORE POSTING: Computer conferencing implies structured communication, but much confusion results when learners contribute postings in the incorrect areas. Review the structure of your posting and check the conference you are posting to.

The following topics are discussion forums that have been created in the Learner Lounge Area. This area is for anyone to share informal personal accounts, social events, and other information not essential to the class.

- *Introducing yourself:* Introduce yourself to the class in this forum. Share information about your job, family, or hobbies.

- *Clarifying issues:* Use this area to clarify course issues related to technology, readings, or assignments.

- *Share "almost" anything:* Use this area to share strategies, fun activities, or anything related to the course.

- *Group discussion summaries:* Please place your discussion summaries for each unit in this topic area.

- *Posting of team tasks:* Use this area to post final team tasks per unit, so everyone in the course can view the team contributions.

PROVIDE INSIGHTFUL COMMENTS: Computer conferencing invites everyone to discuss exciting issues in a way that uniquely evolves. Because the group synergy is greater than any one person's thoughts could be alone, an effective posting does more than provide agreement to a comment. An effective posting does not monopolize the conversation. Rather, it adds something, states the author's position, and solicits a response.

LIMIT THE LENGTH OF YOUR POSTINGS: The typical message should be no more than a screen in length, or three paragraphs. If it is more than two screens, people will get lost and probably not read it all the way through. The key is to limit your contribution to one key idea with supporting points and only one question. If you have more ideas or questions you want to ask others, place each in separate postings. Otherwise, you will confuse the conversation.

USE GOOD NETIQUETTE:

- Check the discussion frequently, respond appropriately, and stay on subject.

- Provide a little background on yourself the first time you enter the discussion. For example, "My name is Mary Peterson, and I am the Program Manager of the Young People of America in My city, My state. My question is. …" or, "The most pressing issue my staff faces is. …"

- Personalize your question or response. Address your message to the person by using his or her name, for example, "Mary, thanks for your suggestions on professional development opportunities for directors."

- Be specific. Identify what issue, topic, or specific statement you are asking about or responding to.

- Focus on one subject per message. It is hard to answer a question like, "I was wondering what you thought about online learning, the technology tools for online instruction, and what to do about using learning management systems." Better to ask a specific question about one of these broad topics to start a "conversation."

- Refer to the topic or message you are replying to by including the topic in your message. For example, "Hi, this is Mary again, I'm following up on the comment that was made by John about the history of distance education."

- Invite a response to your comment by asking another open-ended question. For example, "… so that's what they do in this online program. What strategies have worked in other institutions that use online education?"

Continued

- No SHOUTING!—Capitalize words only to highlight a point or for titles.

- Be professional and use care when interacting online; you don't have the ability to gauge a person's reaction or feelings as you do in a face-to-face conversation.

- Use humor carefully—it is equally hard to gauge a reaction to your funny comment or aside—and the recipient may misinterpret your attempt to be funny as criticism.

- Identify your sources if you use quotes, references, or resources.

- Keep messages brief—no more than two or three paragraphs at a time. (Any longer and it becomes difficult to read, so plan your responses before you write them. And shorter messages encourage more people to join in the discussion.) If you do post a long message, warn other readers at the beginning that it is lengthy.

- Never share someone's posting to someone else without getting permission first.

Join in and have fun!
I am looking forward to seeing you all online!
Your Instructor

Included in the sample scavenger hunt is the completion of an individual data sheet and a Getting-to-Know-You Survey. Exhibit 4.3 provides a sample individual data sheet. Exhibit 4.4 provides a sample Getting-to-Know-You Survey. This kind of survey is widely used by online programs and is freely available online. You may find it online under the name "Are You Ready for Online Learning?" We have adapted some of its elements and renamed it to give it a more personal feel.

Exhibit 4.3
Sample Individual Data Sheet

Course Name, Number, Year of Instruction

INDIVIDUAL DATA SHEET

Name _____

Home Address _____

City _____ State _____ Zip _____

e-mail address _____

Occupation (title and name of
employer) _____

Business address

_____

City _____ State _____ Zip _____

Phone (Business) _____ (Home) _____

Degrees held and
major _____

Degree for which you are now
working _____

What would you like to achieve in this course?

_____

Exhibit 4.4
Getting-to-Know-You Survey

THE PURPOSE OF THIS SURVEY IS TO HELP ME LEARN A LITTLE ABOUT YOU. AFTER COMPLETING THE SURVEY, PLEASE SUBMIT YOUR ANSWERS.

1. Having face-to-face interaction is:

   Not particularly important

   Somewhat important to me

   Very important to me

2. I would classify myself as someone who:

   Often gets things done ahead of time

   Needs reminding to get things done on time

   Puts things off until the last minute

3. When an instructor hands out directions for an assignment, I prefer:

   Figuring out the instructions myself

   Trying to follow the directions on my own, then asking for help as needed

   Having the instructions explained to me

4. I need the instructor to constantly remind me of due dates and assignments

   Rarely

   Sometimes

   Often

5. Considering my professional and personal schedule, the amount of time I have for an online course is:

   More than for a campus course

   The same as for a class on campus

   Less than for a class on campus

6. When I am asked to use e-mail, computers, or other new technologies presented to me:

   I look forward to learning new skills.

   I feel apprehensive, but try anyway.

   I put it off or try to avoid it.

7. As a reader, I would classify myself as:

   Good—I usually understand the text without help.

   Average—I sometimes need help to understand the text.

   Below average—I often need help to understand the text.

8. If I have to go to campus to take exams or complete work:

I have difficulty getting to campus, even in the evenings and on weekends.

I may miss some lab assignments or exam deadlines if campus labs are not open on evenings and weekends.

I can go to campus at any time.

9. I am a self-directed, self-motivated, independent learner who will ask for help from the instructor when necessary:

Yes

No

10. I have good reading and writing skills for getting directions and information and for completing assignments:

Yes

No

11. I have basic computer experience and competence with word processing and Internet browser software:

Yes

No

12. I have regular access to the computer I will use to connect to the online course:

Yes

No

13. I know how to send and receive e-mail:

Yes

No

14. I know how to attach documents to e-mail:

Yes

No

15. I can use the Internet to find information and resources:

Yes

No

16. I can download files to my hard drive:

Yes

No

Continued

THE PURPOSE OF THIS SURVEY IS TO HELP ME LEARN A LITTLE ABOUT YOU. AFTER COMPLETING THE SURVEY, PLEASE SUBMIT YOUR ANSWERS.

What is your current employment, if employed? How many years of professional experience do you have?

What are your future career goals?

What is your learner status (full/part-time)?

What is/are the reason(s) for enrolling in this online course?

What are your goals for this online course?

What would you like to share about yourself to help me get to know you better?

When he designed his course, Carlos created and uploaded his orientation materials to the learning management system. Remember, however, that just creating orientation materials and uploading them are not all that need to happen for learners to feel that they are "there" and "together." Follow-up on learner access to the materials, clarification of course structure and expectations through open forums, and encouragement via personal e-mails and general group announcements are necessary at the beginning of the course. As mentioned, this is the critical moment when novice learners tend to become discouraged and drop the course because instructor presence is not "there."

Biographical Sharing   Another orientation activity is the biographical form (Exhibit 4.5), in which you and your learners share, in a systematic way, a picture with a name and personal information about educational history, memberships in professional organizations, publication history, professional awards and honors, hobbies and interests, and personal contact information. These forms may then be compiled into a biographical booklet with everyone's information for easy download. This is a good strategy for bringing the learners and the instructor closer to each other. Carlos, for example, could focus this activity on the communications field by having learners share the professional experiences that they bring to the course and name the organizations they have joined. When they do this activity early in the course, learners begin to network, relate to each other, and experience a sense of (professional) presence.

When the learners in a course are educators themselves, they may create an educator autobiography that includes information about their first teaching experiences, how they became teachers, what has worked well for them in the teaching roles they have had in the past, and how they have arrived at their current positions. To expand this activity, ask learners to create a PowerPoint slide that summarizes what teaching means for them individually; then have them share it with the rest of the class in the discussion area. If learners are not currently teaching, they can share information about their education instead. To create an interactive experience with a sense of presence, encourage your learners to comment on each others' postings for similarities and differences in experiences. You may also want to be part of the slide sharing and discussion.

Ice-Breakers A useful strategy to encourage relationships among course participants is to use ice-breakers. Three examples of online ice-breakers are the Virtual License Plate (Exhibit 4.6), Where in the World Are You? (Exhibit 4.7), and What Do You Like? (Exhibit 4.8). These ice-breakers give your learners an opportunity to creatively share personal information with the other course members.

Exhibit 4.6
Virtual License Plate

This activity can be used to help learners and instructors learn about each other in a creative way. It is an excellent ice-breaker activity for the first week in an online course.

For this activity, a license plate template is posted in the learning management system for learners to download. The instructor asks learners to draw numbers, letters, short phrases, pictures, and/or symbols in a creative way inside it to design a virtual license plate. The plate's purpose is to tell something about themselves, their families, their pets, their work, their hobbies, or their other interests. Instructors create license plates too. The instructor and learners then upload these to the learning management system for sharing. This helps both learners and the instructor build a sense of presence and feel connected to a community. A variation on the Virtual License Plate is the creation of a vanity website. A vanity website is a template of a website with specific topics (name, school, education, family, hobbies, and so on) to describe personal information.

Exhibit 4.7
Where in the World Are You?

This activity helps learners visualize where everyone in their class is located. It is an excellent activity to use in the first part of the course.

   In this activity, a flat map is provided and learners mark their location(s) on the map. The flat map may be of a city, state, a country, or the world. Everyone gains a sense of the geographical spread of their classmates. The map can be posted to the learning management system and downloaded by the learners. After the learners mark the map they upload it to share. Information about their location, culture, and traditions can also be included.

Exhibit 4.8
What Do You Like?

This activity will bring a smile to learners' faces. It too is an excellent ice-breaker for the beginning of a course to help learners become involved.

What Is Your Favorite Cake?

- Chocolate
- Vanilla
- Strawberry
- Marble
- Carrot
- Cheese cake

Continued

- Hickory nut

- German chocolate

- Other

Explain why: _____

As can be seen, learners download a poll that asks about their favorite cake flavor. They check their favorite cake or add a cake and then explain why it's their favorite. Then they post it to the learning management system to share. A variation of this activity is "I would like to take a trip to. ..." or "My favorite pizza topping is. ..." A polling program could also be used and inserted into the learning management system survey feature.

Getting to Know Your Group or Team If the online course includes cooperative and collaborative work, you may want to assign learners to a small group or team (five to seven members) at the beginning of the course and engage them in a getting-to-know-your-group or -team activity. Groups focus on cooperative individual learning. In small groups, learners can get to know each other and come up with a group name that represents the group's characteristics; they can determine group rules and identify task timelines.

The point of a team is for its members to work collaboratively with each other to accomplish a common goal. When assigning learners to teams, you may decide on team makeup based on diversity of gender, culture, or field of study; online experience; knowledge of the subject; and learning style preferences. A more diverse team makeup has the potential to provide a richer experience for learners. In order to create a sense of presence in group or teamwork, guidelines for facilitation can be provided. Exhibit 4.9 suggests facilitation techniques for creating a sense of presence during group or teamwork.

Groups and teamwork are ideal in courses that focus on communication and leadership skills because they prepare learners to function in a cooperative and collaborative setting that resembles the real world. As we have already seen, without the kinds of cues that are evident in the physical world, doing this is a more complex activity that requires intentional design. In this activity, learners themselves are the group or team facilitators. For this reason, you, as the instructor, should provide this type of instruction to them, before the class begins.

Exhibit 4.9
Facilitating Online Group or Team Activities

Facilitating Online Group or Team Activities

This online course will provide opportunities for group or team activities in two different ways:

1. Online group discussion

2. Online team project

Both types of activities will involve facilitation of some sort; each requires different facilitation skills. The focus of the online group discussion is individual learning; the focus of the online team project is teamwork. Each member of the team may at one point or another take on the role of facilitator. Here's how you can successfully facilitate these activities.

Facilitating Online Group Discussion

To effectively facilitate an online discussion, you need to focus on providing the structure and tone for the conversations. You should set a friendly and safe forum for discussion. Start the discussion with a message welcoming everyone to the discussion unit (identify unit, topics, and/or readings), state the purpose and organization of the online discussion period, and then ask a question related to the readings.

Facilitators of online group discussions must guide the discussion. They need to use techniques that will get the discussion started and then keep it on track. Participation in the discussion needs to be encouraged in a variety of ways. The facilitator will need to ask questions and encourage participants to be thoughtful about their responses and promote sharing of ideas and information. Here are some functions the facilitator may perform when facilitating the discussion:

Contextualizing Functions

- Open the discussions by announcing the theme of the discussion; share experiences or symbols (i.e., emoticons) to clarify content and purpose.

Continued

- Set group norms.
- Set an agenda for the discussion.

Monitoring Functions

- Recognize participants' ideas to assure them that their contribution is valued and welcome, or to correct any misapprehensions about the context of the discussion.
- Solicit comments from participants.

Meta Functions

- To remedy problems in context, avoid any information overload.
- Summarize the state of the discussion to find unifying threads in the participants' comments. This type of function encourages and implicitly prompts participants to pursue their ideas.

Facilitating Online Team Projects

To facilitate a team project, you will need to use techniques to encourage team rapport and activities. Each team participant is different, so different approaches are needed to achieve the desired results. Expectations for participation must be very clear. Team members need to know what the facilitator expects from them and what they can expect from the facilitator. Here are some guidelines for facilitating a team project:

- Define the amount and frequency of time that each team member will spend online.
- Consider having a facilitator for each team project task.
- Develop team ground rules for deadlines, postings, editing of the project, roles and responsibilities, etc.
- Set the team expectations at the beginning of the team process and review them periodically during the course.

DURING THE ONLINE COURSE

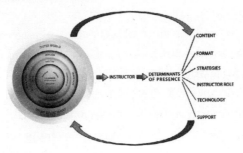

Determinants of Presence

When you design activities to be carried out during the course, you will take the same approach as you did when designing experiences that take place before the course. Table 4.2 describes this process.

Course Activities

To maintain a sense of presence during the online course, you will want to intentionally involve learners in interactive activities: you with your learners, learners and learners with you, and learners with learners in a group or team. If the format of the learning experience is self-paced, the interactive activities should focus on one-on-one with your learners. A variety of activities can be incorporated into this sequence of the course: instructor-led activities, logistical and instructional activities, cooperative activities, and collaborative activities.

Instructor-Led Activities

Instructor-led activities are initiated by the instructor with the purpose of communicating information, assessing performance, monitoring learner progress, and helping create a sense of presence. They include announcements; electronic office hours; support, mentoring and tutoring, feedback on assignments, and electronic portfolio feedback.

Announcements   Interactions between you and your learners help maintain continuity and flow and support your learners' needs. You can continue to maintain presence during the course by making announcements. They may take the form of text messages via e-mail or audio, video, or text notices posted on the learning management system, social networking sites, or handheld devices. Weekly or biweekly announcements give learners a sense of your presence throughout the course and keep them on task. Exhibit 4.10 provides a sample announcement script that can also be used as a video or text e-mail message reminder. Notice that this announcement provides directions, explains course unit requirements, shows and offers support for learners as they enter the first unit in the course, and nicely reminds them of tasks they may have not yet completed. Also note that the language of the announcement is conversational and personal.

For learners who constantly check e-mail on a computer or handheld device, e-mail announcements can serve as reminders for course activities, communication, and task log. Learners who prefer having a one-stop space for the online

Table 4.2
Determinants of Presence: During the Online Course

DETERMINANTS	DESCRIPTION
Content	The type and focus of the content for your online course depends on the discipline you are teaching (education, math, history, etc.). You should decide which focus works best for your online course: content, process, or a mix of both.
Format	The format of your learning activities will vary depending on the objectives and outcomes of your course. For example, your course may focus heavily on content and require learners to work independently. Or it may focus on the creation of a product and require learners to work collaboratively in teams. Or it might be a blend of both formats to offer a more diverse experience. Your decision is key at this point, before you begin creating your course strategies.
Strategies	You may use a variety of strategies to create presence during the online course: online group discussion forums, team projects, debates, fishbowl, mini-lectures, PowerPoint with voiceover, short video sequences, synchronous Web or videoconferencing, guest experts, chat, object or picture demonstration, collaborative concept maps, participant videos, virtual lab work or simulations, blog participation, interviews, and trigger videos. This list is not all-inclusive. You may think of other activities to include in your online course.
Role of instructor	You will take different roles during the online course: designer of activities as the course evolves, facilitator of group discussions, catalyst for interactions, observer, evaluator, mentor, and tutor. During the course, you may also provide emotional and psychological support for your learners.

DETERMINANTS	DESCRIPTION
Technology	If you are teaching with a learning management system, this online environment should be a one-stop location for the course, but it does not take away from using other technologies to increase a sense of presence. For example, video announcements at the beginning of each unit, event simulations using Second Life®, wikis, blogs, Twitter, and other social networking tools can be used to enhance a sense of presence and provide opportunities for your learners to become familiar with new tools.
Support	Technical support should always be available to you and your learners. This is especially important when you are using new technologies and software. You want to make sure your learners know the help desk support services available through your organization. Otherwise, you will have to provide constant technical support. Support can also take the form of learner-to-learner assistance by creating areas where they can help each other. Instructional support can take the form of providing general assistance to all learners through tutoring and mentoring. You also need to pay attention to learners with special needs by adapting course materials and following up with them.

Exhibit 4.10
Sample Announcement Script

Welcome to Unit 1!

Unit 1 starts today. If you are still having issues with your login to the course, please contact me right away. Many of you have already completed the scavenger hunt. This is great! Your contributions have already added a lot to the course.

A Few Tips

Go to the Content area and select Unit 1. Review the Unit Overview. You will find there details about the readings, study guides, and templates for your team project and online group discussions.

Continued

Activities That Create a Sense of Presence

Readings

There are required and suggested readings. Make your priority the required readings. If you have time, go on to the suggested readings. Some of you may not have the textbook yet, so do the e-Reserve readings first for Unit 1.

Study Guides

There are four files in the Study Guides area. You may want to download the files and review them. These files provide summaries of your readings.

Templates

There are five template files that will help you work on your team project. You may want to download them.

Online Group Discussions

You may want to determine the group roles before starting the discussions. I am flexible this week, so get the group roles rolling right away and then the facilitator should post a few questions to start the discussions. The online group discussions will continue until next week.

Hint for facilitators: If you have never been a facilitator before, check the following PowerPoint files in the orientation area for tips: "How to Ask Online Questions" and "How to Participate in Online Discussions."

Individual Data Sheet

If you have not completed the Individual Data Sheet yet, there is still time to upload it to the drop box in the learning management system.

I am looking forward to reading your insights during this unit. If you are confused, don't understand my directions, or need any type of help, feel free to contact me via e-mail or telephone.

See you online!

Your Instructor

course will find it more convenient to use the announcement area in the learning management system. Learners who prefer hearing or seeing you will appreciate an audio or video announcement posted in the learning management system, on a social networking website, or downloaded to a handheld device in audio or video format. Learners may also follow brief statements about the course through

---

Exhibit 4.11
Sample Twitter Announcement

What are you doing?   140

Check new simulation file in LMS for Unit 2 ... exciting new
material!

tweet

Twitter. Using all of these social networking tools might seem overwhelming to you. It is your choice to select and use those most appropriate to your online course. Carlos decided to use two methods for his announcements: biweekly video announcements and a social networking environment. If you are not sure which method will work for you, consider polling your learners at the beginning of the course to identify their favorite communication tools.

Using different technologies to communicate with learners not only creates a greater sense of presence but also serves as an opportunity to learn new communication technologies. Exhibit 4.11 shows a sample social networking announcement using Twitter. Note that this announcement is brief and directs learners to check something new and exciting about the course.

Electronic Office Hours   Electronic office hours are another way to create presence through the objective experiences of text, audio, or video. You can set specific times during the week when you will be available for your learners' course questions or needs for clarification. Electronic office hours allow you and your learners to feel as if you are psychologically and physically together. It is important to consider learners' time zones when scheduling the hours; set at least two different times so you can meet their needs. You may use a variety of technologies to connect with your learners synchronously and asynchronously. For example,

Skype offers its users opportunities to interact via text chat, audio, or video, as in the case of Carlos. In Second Life®, in addition to connecting via text and audio, users can have an immersive experience as avatars. Facebook, MySpace, and Twitter offer a more public forum for communication with learners. You can identify which media you feel are most appropriate. As previously mentioned, your learners can also help you decide which one to use. It is a good idea to have more than one option.

Instructor Support, Mentoring, and Tutoring Activities   Teaching online means instructor support, mentoring, and tutoring; all of these add to the sense of presence. General support for learners is an ongoing task for the instructor throughout the course, and it includes both instructional and technical support, as previously mentioned.

Instructor support also means assisting learners with special needs. Learners who require special consideration in the adaptation of course materials may interact with you in different ways from other learners. For example, blind learners may require adaptive technology such as audio recording of your lectures or audio feedback on their individual assignments. Deaf learners may prefer to interact with the assistance of an interpreter during synchronous interaction with you when they are less comfortable with text interaction. In each case, you need to plan, adapt, and schedule ahead of time.

For more information about special needs learners, refer to the website http://people.rit.edu/easi/ and the book *Information Access and Adaptive Technology,* by Cunningham and Coombs (1997). The website will keep you up-to-date on current technologies and strategies in this area. The book is a practical guide to help instructors design an online environment conducive to learners with special needs, including infrastructure, support, planning, special technology, and examples of model programs.

Mentoring involves a trusted developmental relationship between you and your learners to foster learner personal growth throughout the online course. Mentoring learners online can create a sense of presence, especially to support novice and marginalized learners (Burgess, 2007). First-time online learners are likely to feel insecure both technologically and academically due to course design and delivery methods that involve autonomy and self-directedness. One-on-one mentoring meetings will help these learners feel more comfortable. These meetings can give you the time to listen to their concerns and offer feedback on how to be disciplined and become confident in this new environment. Marginalized learners tend to place themselves at the margin of the course when they are in a face-to-face situation, and these kinds of feelings may transfer to the online environment. You need to be aware of them. Personal interaction with you and mentoring will help such learners feel more comfortable about their online experience over time.

Tutoring involves helping learners improve their learning strategies to promote independence and empowerment and is another way to foster presence online. Learners who feel that they need extra assistance with learning strategies on how to gain knowledge of course concepts may require personal tutoring from you. Your tutoring role is to assist learners in helping themselves become independent individuals in the online environment. Tutoring may take place during electronic office hours or at special times scheduled by you and your learners.

As we saw at the beginning of this chapter, Carlos was entirely aware that his role as an instructor in an online environment involved a different frame of mind. He knew he had to feel, think, and behave in new ways to incorporate a sense of presence. By including support, mentoring, and tutoring activities, he could better manage the instructional process for his learners. As for learners like Amanda, feelings of isolation, frustration, and dissatisfaction can be easily resolved with instructor support, mentoring, and tutoring.

Feedback on Assignments   Offering feedback to your learners can create a form of presence as you provide constructive comments about participation, tasks, and performance. These comments can be expressed through positive reinforcement and praise, clear explanation of assignments, or constructive advice on how your learners should function in your course. If feedback needs to be individual, you may want to use a drop box or a grading feature in the learning management system. Providing individual feedback on assignments in the online environment is not that different from doing so in a face-to-face class. The difference may merely be in the amount of detail provided due to the lack of physical presence.

Electronic Portfolio Feedback   You may want to provide feedback through the use of an electronic portfolio (e-portfolio), either within the learning management system or through a third-party software program. Your learners can collect and document artifacts and reflect on their learning progress in the course. Your interactions with your learners will serve as feedback for self-development during the course while also helping to create a sense of presence.

Logistical and Instructional Activities

When the format of the learning experience is group-based rather than self-paced, creating group presence is essential. Group presence functions on at least two levels: logistical and instructional.

Logistical Presence Logistical activities involve interactions your learners have among themselves and with you in non-content-related discussion forums (Schmidt & Conceição, 2008). During these interactions, you and your learners can post "housekeeping" messages related to the mechanics of the online course. Learners can also ask questions and locate information about course materials or technology features on the learning management system. In the scavenger hunt example provided in Exhibit 4.2, learners are instructed to participate in two forums that are for non-content-related postings: "Clarifying Issues" and "Share 'Almost' Anything." In the beginning of the chapter, we saw that Amanda was taking a leadership role in the "Share 'Almost' Anything" forum; such forums enable both learners and instructors a way to help others and share information.

Instructional Presence Instructional activities can take the form of a one-way instructor content presentation to learners, as Carlos did at the beginning of this chapter, and one-way learner sharing of course materials with other learners and you. One-way instructor content presentation can occur through mini-lectures, guest lectures, and object or picture demonstration. Table 4.3 explains how these activities may be used to create presence in your online course. One-way asynchronous instructor-content presentation activities may seem intimidating— because you may feel your learners do not need you at all—but this is only an impression. You must still feel, think, and behave as if you were "there" with your learners when you make prerecordings. If you are dissatisfied with this kind of delayed instruction, you can always use live one-way presentations via chat, audio, and video.

Table 4.3

Examples of One-Way Instructor Content Presentation Activities

ACTIVITY	DESCRIPTION
Mini-lectures	Mini-lectures are short, ten- to fifteen-minute presentations using PowerPoint with voiceover, short video sequences, or synchronous Web or videoconferencing.
Guest experts	Similar to instructor mini-lectures, these are made by a guest expert who you may invite to present a topic in a lecture format. In both cases, chat via text interaction may enhance a sense of presence.
Object or picture demonstration	Object or picture demonstration involves the development and posting of a video illustration—for example, a work of art. The video could begin with an instructor introduction about the assignment using conversational language and then directing learners to the task to be accomplished.

One-way learner sharing of course materials involves individual learning with interaction with other learners and with you. Examples of this kind of activity include creating concept maps, participant videos, virtual labwork or simulations, architectural software, blog participation, interviews, and trigger videos. Table 4.4 explains how one-way learner activities can be used in your online course. These activities can create a sense of presence through sharing individual work and provide opportunities for the development of leadership skills as in the case of Amanda.

Cooperative Activities

You may also involve learners in online activities that are either cooperative or collaborative. For example, cooperative activities may involve learners participating in a group discussion in which they share, discuss, and synthesize ideas or concepts on a specific topic. Individual thought, emotion, and behavior affect the online learning experience of group members through diverse intellectual contributions, passionate perspectives, and individual performances. Although learners work together in this kind of group situation, their learning may be assessed individually. Cooperation is essential in group learning. Examples of

Table 4.4

Examples of One-Way Learner Sharing of Course Materials

ACTIVITY	DESCRIPTION
Concept maps	Concept maps are graphical representations drawn by learners to show their understanding of a set of concepts. Your learners can create their own concept map of a reading or book chapter to synthesize information, share it in the discussion area with others, and engage in an exchange of ideas about similarities and differences of interpretations. Concept maps can be created using software programs such as Inspiration®, CmapTools, etc.
Participant videos	Your learners may create a video of their own teaching and share it with others for performance feedback. The video file can be uploaded to the drop box or shared in a general forum area in the learning management system.
Labwork	Learners can participate in labwork under your facilitation, using virtual lab software to experiment with math formulas and chemical reactions or practice a foreign language. Learners can then share their results or lab experiences with others in the general forum area of the learning management system.
Architectural software	Using architecture software, you can guide your learners through a simulated "design-and-build" process that provides them with an immersive experience. In a similar fashion to labwork, learners can share their experiences through the process in the general forum area of the learning management system.
Blogs	Blogs can be used as an electronic journal or a space for a discussion forum. When used as electronic journals, your learners record their reflections and share with others. Through the comment area in a blog, others share their insights on a topic that will lead to a discussion.
Interviews	Your learners can individually question a person on a topic or issue and present a summary of their findings to the rest of the class. Then they can comment on each other's interview techniques and outcomes in the general forum area of the learning management system.
Trigger videos	Trigger videos involve your learners selecting a thirty-second to three-minute video segment to challenge other learners to discuss an issue related to class content. Then, learners share their insights with each other in the general forum area of the learning management system.

activities that require cooperation among learners in a group include group discussion on course content, debates, and fishbowl.

Group Discussions   In group discussions, learners take on the roles of facilitator, contributor, or summarizer. The facilitator is responsible for initiating the discussion with one or two questions about the readings. As group members respond to the facilitator's questions, the facilitator extends the discussion by posing new questions on issues that arise out of the discussion. The summarizer is responsible for providing a brief review of the main issues discussed, the key points that participants made in their group, and any conclusions reached by the group at the end of the discussion. All learners are contributors and are required to respond to questions posted by both facilitators and other group members, as well as to review and comment on the responses of others. Group discussions give learners the opportunity to analyze course content and extend their knowledge through interaction with their group. This process can add to the group sense of presence.

Debates   Debates have similarities with group discussions, but follow different procedures. Debates foster critical thinking and analysis. You may assign debate participants a position addressing a particular question. Learners submit their position (pro or con) by a specific day, refute in two days, and rebut in another two days. This type of activity involves group work where learners work in small groups of four or six. One person, the summarizer, reports the results of the group discussions. Your role is to monitor and keep the discussions on track.

Fishbowl   In a fishbowl activity, learners are assigned to three separate groups. The first group discusses the selected topic or issue during a specified time frame, the second summarizes and reports on the first group's discussion, and the third observes the discussion and adds to the report created by the second group. This process provides an expanded perspective on a particular topic or issue, involves learners in cooperative work, and stimulates a sense of presence.

Collaborative Activities

In collaborative activities your learners are responsible for developing a team project or product. Collaboration can take the form of task completion and final presentation of a project or product. In collaborative interactions, learners tend to assign roles and responsibilities for the developmental tasks. Collaboration is key to team learning. Team members must consider learners who live in different time zones and have different cultural perspectives, diverse family and work responsibilities, and different collaborative styles. Projects may include developing a program or creating a script. Products may include a report on the results of an experiment or creation of an online resource book. A variety of technologies may be used to bring team members together to brainstorm, discuss, develop, refine, and present the project or product. Wikis, blogs, Twitter, Second Life®, and other social networking tools are examples of Internet-based technologies that facilitate teamwork collaboration. In collaborative teamwork, members are often assessed as a team rather than individually. Three examples of collaborative activities include case studies, digital storytelling, and virtual team projects.

Case Studies Case studies vary in type from discipline to discipline. A case study may be given to four library studies learners, who are asked to work on it first on their own, then together as a team, and present the results to the rest of the class through a summary. Nursing learners might read a legal case, discuss it in their team, solve the legal case, and then report the results. Business management learners can get together in teams via synchronous chat to discuss a case study on ethics. A workplace learning course may use a case study with the class divided into four or five teams. Learners look at a case study in an article. Here, you might ask each team to elect someone to take minutes of the discussion and someone to report back the team's discussion to the larger class (Conceição-Runlee, 2001). Your role is as a facilitator for these teams.

Digital Storytelling In digital storytelling, the team identifies a topic and then collaboratively works on a script, creating the narrative and taking camera shots. Afterward, each team member is assigned a role of talent (actors), production crew (camera, microphone), and post-production crew (editing). The final product may be posted in the learning management system or the public YouTube site.

Virtual Team Projects You can place your learners in virtual teams to create projects in a 3-D environment such as the Second Life® virtual world. In the first part of the activity, learners can visit organizations in Second Life® and gather information to use in their project. Then, they meet synchronously in the virtual world to brainstorm, discuss, and create communication plans for starting a new organization in the virtual world. Finally, the virtual teams present their plans to the whole class and receive feedback from you and the other teams based on feasibility, creativity, and return on investment. This entire process can take place in Second Life®.

All these cooperative and collaborative activities can enhance a sense of presence in any online course that involves a group-based format. For example, group discussions, debates, and case studies can create a social experience in which learners communicate and interact with each other or with animated characters. This happens through personal and emotional connection to the group with the purpose of accomplishing a task. In this case, the instructor's presence can be made known through guidance and formative feedback.

END OF THE COURSE

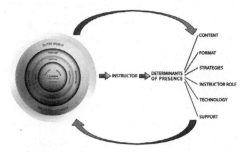

Determinants of Presence

We include the final two to three weeks of the course in this last sequence of activities. Your instructor presence may lessen at this time because learners are more independent, confident, and focused on what they need to do to complete the course (Conceição, Baldor, & Desnoyers, 2009). Table 4.5 describes how the determinants of presence are used in the last sequence of the online course.

Course Activities

To maintain the flow of the online course and help learners complete their final tasks, give special attention to the communication between you and them, create

Table 4.5

Determinants of Presence: End of the Online Course

DETERMINANTS	DESCRIPTION
Content	The type of content for your online course remains the same as that used during the course. However, at this point the focus is on completing tasks and assignments and finalizing projects.
Format	The format of your learning activities should remain the same as that used during the course. You may consider decreasing the amount of readings when learners are completing tasks and assignments.
Strategies	The strategies may remain the same as the ones used during the course, depending on your course, but the intensity is likely to decrease. Guiding learners to conclude course tasks, providing feedback, and communicating about final projects and assignments are important to maintain the flow of the course and help learners complete the course effectively.
Role of instructor	Your role now is to clarify issues through announcements, provide support through individual and group or team meetings, and assess final tasks and assignments.
Technology	The technology remains the same. You may place feedback on assignments and performance in the gradebook of the learning management system.
Support	Technology should be totally transparent by now unless there are technical problems in the system.

an environment for group or team feedback, design constructive feedback on assignment performance, and provide a venue for course closure.

End-of-Course Communication   One-way communication through announcements has been an important aspect of presence throughout Carlos's online course. At the end of the course, your instructions should guide your learners to complete tasks, projects, and assignments. At this point, learners may feel overwhelmed by the number of activities they need to complete. Your announcements should direct learners to specific tasks, deadlines, and requirements so that they feel more in control of what they need to accomplish, rather than focusing on the big picture. In a regular face-to-face course, you might announce the final course tasks the day before the last day of class. In contrast, in an online course you need to plan your final announcements and reminders ahead of time or it will be too late for your learners to meet their deadlines. Doing so shows your concern for your learners, helps maintain consistent course management on your part, and continues your sense of presence until the end of the course.

Exhibit 4.12 provides a sample end-of-course announcement. It not only reminds learners what needs to be completed but directs them to specific areas of the learning management system and provides general comments on a previous assignment. It is task-oriented and personal, shows instructor support, and helps create a sense of presence. Another important point that the letter makes is to let learners know that feedback is available in the gradebook. This information can reduce learners' anxiety about their performance.

Your last announcement to your learners is just as important as the others you have sent because your last communication can bring closure to your online course. If the course ends during the holiday season, a personal holiday message can create a feeling of community and presence. See Exhibit 4.13 for a sample final course holiday announcement. It expresses the instructor's personal feelings about the online course. It indicates that the course was challenging and that everyone (including the instructor) has learned a lot from it. In addition, it says that the course will have an effect on the learners' experience long after the course is over. Finally, it also shows learners where to find their final grades and wishes them a happy holiday season. The postscript encourages the learners to continue communicating with each other even after the course is over, giving them the sense that presence can continue.

At this point, group or team activities are being finalized. Strategies used during the online course may remain the same, but other examples of assignments appropriate for this portion of the course include learners' critique of each other's papers, team project presentations with self- and peer feedback, and whole-group discussion of a final topic.

Paper Critique   This activity may take the form of a final course paper in which learners create individual synthesis of a specific topic and share it with their small group. Each individual in the group is assigned two papers to critique and

Exhibit 4.12
Sample End-of-Course Announcement

SUBJECT: Welcome to the Last Unit!

Hello everyone—

Welcome to the last Unit in the course! There are still a few things to complete:

- *Prototype evaluation:* The evaluation of the prototype course each team created starts tomorrow. I am giving you access to the site to do the prototype evaluation today. I am asking everyone to complete the review by Friday. Please post your review in the drop box.

- *Final team presentation:* Your final team presentation should be completed with revisions after the prototype evaluation. The course outline states that this assignment should be completed in five days, but I will give you ten days to make any modifications to the project.

- *Unit 6 feedback:* I have already posted feedback in the course management system for Unit 6. I am impressed with the level of quality of the assignments. You all did well!!!

- *Team and self-evaluation:* You must complete the team and self-evaluation by the last week of class. For this requirement, you need to download the evaluation template, save it to your computer, work on the template (comments on each team member and self are required), and then upload it to the drop box.

Let me know if you have any questions. I can meet with any team to clarify any issues.

See you online!

Your Instructor

SUBJECT: Happy Holidays!

Hello everyone—

It has been a pleasure working with all of you. You made my life easier during the course. This online course is an intense course and requires a huge effort on the part of learners and instructor. But I have learned throughout the years that efforts are never in vain. You will use your learning and the experience with your group and team as you continue your work in the program or an outside program, your new job after you graduate, or as a part of your life.

I have posted the grades in the learning management system and will post final grades by Friday. If you find that I missed anything, please let me know.

I enjoyed reading your insights throughout the course and reviewing your assignments. I have learned a lot from you too.

Happy Holidays!

Your Instructor

PS: I will keep the learning management system site up for a while, so feel free to exchange messages with each other there as long as you want.

---

comment on. After receiving feedback, they make revisions and then submit final paper to the instructor. This type of assignment creates a sense of peer presence through support.

Team Project Self- and Peer Feedback   Having worked together in small teams throughout the course, learners should have already felt a sense of team presence by accomplishing tasks together. One activity to conclude the team assignment is to ask learners to provide self- and peer feedback. Exhibit 4.14 shows how this activity can be used to enhance team presence. This type of activity makes participants responsible and accountable for the team tasks from the beginning of the course. Once learners know what is expected of them based on the assignment

Exhibit 4.14
Self- and Peer Feedback

Self- and Peer Feedback

This team project will be based on self- and peer feedback. It will consist of providing yourself and your team members feedback using the following criteria:

- *Intellectual contributions:* a team member's contribution to the content of the project
- *Logistical contributions:* posting, typing, editing, presenting, uploading, etc.
- *Creative contributions:* to the design of the project
- *Leadership contributions:* the driving force behind the operation at one time or another during the project

Note: You should provide comments to substantiate the points you assigned to yourself and other team members.

Scale: 1–5 with 5 high contribution, 1 low contribution

SELF- AND PEER FEEDBACK	POINTS
Intellectual contributions	5
Logistical contributions	5
Creative contributions	5
Leadership contributions	5
Total points (points will be averaged)	20

criteria, they can better understand how a team works collaboratively within a community and increase a sense of presence.

Whole-Group Discussion As we have seen, it is common to assign online learners to small groups that work together throughout the course. A variation of this is the rotation of learners among groups so they can work with and get to know other classmates. You may also consider bringing everyone together at the end of the course for a whole-group discussion of a topic that has implications for the learners' practice in their fields. This discussion can serve as a reflection on what they have learned in the course and offer some perspective on how the information may help them in the future. For example, in an instructional design and teaching strategies course, learners reflect on the role of the instructional designer in an open forum to exchange ideas about how this role is important to their careers. This type of discussion allows them to feel connected to the instructor, the content, and the other learners in the course. Note, however, that when a large group works together, some learners tend to monopolize the discussion and decrease the level of presence of others. Using clear guidelines for participating in large group discussion can help a balanced sense of group presence.

Instructor Feedback Instructor feedback is essential throughout the online course so that learners can sense how they are doing and progressing. Carlos's strategy to put this into practice is to provide individual feedback to his learners when they need it. At the end of the course, the instructor's feedback roles are those of facilitator, supporter, and evaluator. As a facilitator the instructor can clarify issues, provide instructions on assignments and projects, and keep course tasks moving forward. As supporters, instructors can minimize any concerns and counsel learners on how to prioritize tasks. As evaluators, instructors can provide final feedback on team tasks and assess assignments. It is particularly important to provide reasonably prompt feedback to learners, so that they feel less anxious about their course performance. Once Carlos realized that his instructor role in his online course was very different from his role in his face-to-face courses, he adapted his philosophy and teaching strategies. It is important for online instructors to realize when to stay on the sidelines and let learners interact with each other in the learning community.

End-of-the-Course Debriefing For some learners, the end of the course is an overwhelming experience as they assimilate all the content they have covered, the people they interacted with but never physically met, the types of experiences they engaged in online, the different technologies they used, and the ways in which they experienced presence. At this point, a debriefing activity can help learners decompress and process their experience. You may want to create a forum in the general discussion area in which all course participants reflect on the course, share and process feelings, and bring about closure.

It should be noted that the end-of-course activities presented here are not all-inclusive, but they do provide you with examples of strategies that you can use and adapt to your online course.

HOW TO KNOW IF PRESENCE IS "THERE" IN YOUR ONLINE COURSE

As we have seen, presence can be an abstract concept in the online environment. In Chapter 1, we stated that the concept of presence in the online learning experience can be elusive and difficult to understand. Initially, Carlos was not able to understand it. By using the Being There for the Online Learner model and the instructional design framework, you, like Carlos, will be able to create an online course with a sense of presence. Now that you understand how presence can happen in your online course, let's look at how you can find out if presence has really been realized. Through formative (before and during the course) and summative (end-of-course) evaluation methods, you will be able to gather this information. Different approaches to collect this information can be helpful depending on the design of your course.

Note that in this book we do not offer methods for measuring presence in online learning environments; rather, we merely offer strategies to identify ways in which presence has been realized. A more comprehensive look at methods for measuring presence in online courses invites further exploration.

Approaches for Finding Out That Presence Is Realized

How do you know if learners are experiencing a sense of presence in your online course? How do you know if the way you designed your course created a sense of presence? Which content activities and formats incorporated into your online course created a sense of presence? What roles did you play in your online course? What technologies did you use to create a sense of presence? What instructional and technical support did you receive or provide to avoid distractions and create a sense of presence? These questions underline the importance of the determinants of presence that affect the types of experiences and modes of presence that should be intentionally designed into your online course. We suggest the use of a variety of approaches to determine if presence took place in your online course. These approaches include:

- *Learning Management System (LMS) User Progress Report.* One feature of most LMS technologies is a participant progress report with summaries of learner participation (number of postings, access frequency, postings authored, postings read, and so on). This feature allows you to identify which learners have been present and when in your online course. Monitoring for learner presence in the beginning of the course helps you identify lurkers or nonparticipants so you can contact them, clarify course protocols, and offer assistance.

- *Learner participation in orientation activities.* The LMS provides quantitative information about your learners' participation; however, there may be activities that learners have to complete that involve direct communication with you, such as the individual data sheet, biographical form, or surveys. Monitoring for learner participation at the beginning of the course decreases attrition. If learners have a negative first experience with online learning, they are more likely to drop out.

- *Communication log.* Interactions between individual learners and the instructor can be documented and tracked through the use of communication logs such as a drop box, e-mail, survey results in the LMS, and transcripts of postings in the discussion area of the LMS. If the course uses social networking technologies, logs can also be kept on the Web for monitoring and review of presence in your online course.

- *Logistical forum of group or team interactions.* Before the course begins, you may want to engage learners in logistical forums so that the group or team can set guidelines, determine leadership roles, and identify expected timelines for class tasks. These forums can be established in individual group or team areas.

- *General learners and instructor engagement in non-content-related area.* This includes forums such as "Help Desk," "Q&A," "Sharing Resources," and so on. In this area of your online course, you may encourage your learners to post "housekeeping" messages related to the mechanics of your course.

Learners may use this area for asking questions and locating information about course materials or technology features in the LMS.

- *Learner engagement in group or team discussions.* You may want to set up individual group or team areas. Group discussions tend to focus on the course content while team discussions focus on the accomplishment of tasks.

- *Learner mid-course feedback.* Midway through your online course, it is important to check your learners' perceptions and feelings about the course for at least three reasons: doing so shows your concern about your learners, it provides you with information on how the course is progressing, and it gives you an opportunity to better meet your learners' needs. Mid-course feedback can be obtained through the use of critical incidents (Brookfield, 1995), in which learners freely answer open-ended questions. Here are some examples:

  - At what moment in the course did you feel most engaged with what was happening? Why?

  - At what moment in the course did you feel most distanced from what was happening? Why?

  - What action that anyone (you or anyone in your team or class) took in the online environment did you find most affirming and helpful? Why?

  - What action that anyone (you or anyone in your team or class) took in the online environment did you find most puzzling or confusing? Why?

  - What about the online environment during the course surprised you the most? Why?

  - What is the most important thing you learned in the course up to now? Why?

  - Please write one thing that you think still needs clarification

- *Learner engagement in a debriefing forum.* An open forum in the general discussion area can serve as a way for learners to reflect on the course, share and process feelings, and bring about closure at the end of the course.

- *Final course evaluation.* To obtain the learners' perspectives on the overall course sense of presence, you may want to ask them the following questions in a checkbox and open-ended comments format at the end of the course:

BEFORE THE ONLINE COURSE

- What tasks did you complete during the course orientation (i.e., individual data sheet, biographical form, Getting-to-Know-You Survey, visits to content area of LMS, etc.)?

- Please select the types of interactions (with content, with instructor, with other learners, with team members, with technology, etc.) you were involved in before the course began and describe how you were involved. [Instructor: Provide a checkbox here.]

DURING THE ONLINE COURSE

- What communication methods did you use in the course (i.e., telephone, e-mail, fax, LMS, Skype, Second Life®, etc.)?

- Describe how you felt/experienced the following interactions during the course orientation: with content, with instructor, with other learners, with team members, with technology, etc.

- Please select the types of interactions (with content, with instructor, with other learners, with team members, with technology, etc.) you were involved in during the online course and describe how you were involved.

- Please select the types of feedback you received during the course (from the instructor, from team members, from technical support, etc.). Please describe how you felt about them.

- Which type of feedback that you received helped you feel most connected to other participants in the course? Please explain why.

- Please select the types of interactions you had with your instructor during the online course (e-office hours, one-way instructor content presentation, individual assignment interaction, instructor feedback on assignments, course debriefing, etc.). Please describe your feelings of connection.

END OF THE ONLINE COURSE

- At the end of the course, what types of interactions did you participate in (with the instructor, with team members, with other classmates, with technology, etc.)? Please describe how you felt about them.

Table 4.6 provides a summary of approaches, in sequence, that instructors can take to gather information. As we saw at the beginning of this chapter, Carlos decided to use the learning management system for gathering information about his learners during the online course. Until he looked at the information gathered in the learner progress report, he did not realize that his learners were actively engaged in his online course. He also kept a communication log of his interactions with learners as a way to know if his learners were present in his course.

Questions to Ask

When you gather information about your online course, it is a good idea to use a list of questions for each course sequence. Table 4.7 provides questions to guide you in gathering this information. This list will help you determine if you and your learners have experienced a sense of presence in your online course. You may want to add other questions that you feel are appropriate for your particular online course.

Using the Information You Gather

Gathering information before and during the course (formative evaluation) can help you reshape your online course and better meet your learners' needs as your course progresses. Gathering information at the end of the course (summative evaluation) will help you reflect on the types of experiences you used in your course to create a sense of presence. Summative evaluation information can also suggest strategies to enhance your future courses. It is important to note that instructor and learner presence may vary from course to course even when you are teaching the same course. Learners come in with different needs, and your support and presence may change depending on that. In addition, your sense of presence may change over time as you become more comfortable with the online environment, as Carlos did.

Online courses that intentionally incorporate learning activities that create a sense of presence are more likely to be effective than other online courses. However, creating the activities is not everything. All participants in the teaching-learning process must think, feel, and behave with a sense of presence. In the beginning of this chapter, Amanda was actively involved in the course activities and so began to feel that she was part of the online learning community. The online activities designed for her course helped create a sense of presence and

Table 4.6

Approaches for Gathering Information on a Sense of Presence

COURSE SEQUENCE	APPROACHES TO KNOWING PRESENCE IS "THERE"
Before the course begins	• Learning management system user progress report • Learner participation in orientation activities • Communication log between learner and instructor • Logistical forum of group or team interactions • General learners and instructor engagement in non-content-related areas
During the course	• Learning management system user progress report • Communication log between learner and instructor • General learner and instructor engagement in non-content related forums • Learner engagement in group or team discussions • Learner mid-course feedback
End of the course	• Learning management system user progress report • Communication log between learner and instructor • General learner and instructor engagement in non-content-related forums • Learner engagement in group or team discussions • Learner engagement in debriefing forum • Final course evaluation

made her feel that she was "there" and "together" with others. She was so involved in the online course that she was even helping others overcome fears that she had had before.

Carlos has come a long way too. He now thinks differently about the online environment. He realizes that online activities require a different format. The

Table 4.7
Questions to Ask for Determining Presence

COURSE SEQUENCE	QUESTIONS TO ASK
Before the course begins	• How often did learners access the LMS?
	• How many postings were authored and read by each learner?
	• Which forums did the learners post to (how often, how many postings authored, how many postings read)?
	• Which tasks did the learners complete during the orientation?
	• How many messages did the instructor receive from and reply to learners? Which technologies were used?
	• How many postings did the team members author to create team guidelines? Which technologies were used?

During the course

- How often did learners access the LMS?
- How many postings were authored and read by each learner?
- Which content forums did the learners post to (how often, how many postings authored, how many postings read)?
- How many messages did the instructor receive from and respond to learners? Which technologies were used?
- How many postings did the team members author to accomplish tasks? What types of postings did they author? Which technologies were used?
- What other technologies were used during the course to engage learners? How were they used (how often, how many postings authored, how many postings read)?
- How did the learners feel about the course up to this point (refer to earlier critical incident questions)?

Continued

QUESTIONS TO ASK

COURSE SEQUENCE

End of the course

- How often did learners access the LMS?

- How many postings were authored and read by each learner?

- Which content forums did the learners post to (how often, how many postings authored, how many postings read)?

- How many messages did the instructor receive from and respond to learners? Which technologies were used?

- How many postings did the team members author to accomplish tasks? What types of postings did they author? Which technologies did they use?

- What other technologies were used at the end of the course to engage learners? How were they used (how often, how many postings authored, how many postings read)?

- How many learners did participate in the course debriefing forum (how many messages posted, what types of messages authored)?

- How did the learners feel about the overall course experience (refer to earlier final course evaluation questions)?

online course interactions influenced ways in which he related to his learners. He had to rethink his role as an instructor. He began by adapting his lectures to a video format for the online environment, but this resulted in his feeling abandoned and isolated. He resolved these issues by accessing the learning management system progress report. He was thus able to become aware of the fact that his learners were actively involved in the course and were taking a more independent role in the learning process than they did in his face-to-face classes. He also started using different methods to convey his instructor presence, such as Skype, social networking tools, participation in group discussions, and making himself available for individual support when needed.

SUMMARY

In this chapter, we offered activities that can create a sense of presence in your online course based on the potential sequence in which they may be used. We also suggested approaches and questions for gathering information to help you determine if presence is "there" in your online course. Throughout the chapters in this book, we have observed learner Amanda develop and instructor Carlos grow from inexperienced to experienced individuals who are aware of the concept of presence in the online environment. On the part of the instructor, it is also intentional planning and design.

In Chapter 5, we will present three case examples. Each one will address one or more of the three sequences—before the course, during the course, and the end of the course. We then provide a sample syllabus that incorporates a sense of presence. Chapter 5 will end with final thoughts and reflections on future directions for online teaching and learning.

Are You Here or There? Making Sense of Presence

In this chapter, we will present three activity case examples used in online courses. Each includes a description of the activity, activity tasks, how presence was experienced in the course, and approaches to determine if presence happened. The case examples address one or more of the three sequences in an online course: before the course, during the course, and at the end of the course. We will then provide a sample syllabus that incorporates a sense of presence. We will conclude the chapter with our final thoughts on creating a sense of presence in the online environment and future directions.

CASE 1: GETTING TO KNOW YOU AND YOUR COURSE

Activity Description

The purpose of this activity was to help the learners familiarize themselves with the course, with other classmates, and with the course instructor. In the course website, several forums were set up to manage logistical presence (non-content-related course interactions). These interactions dealt with the mechanics of the online classroom and orientation activities.

"Getting to Know You," "Frequently Asked Questions," and "Sharing 'Almost' Anything" were the names of the forums created. In the "Getting to Know You" forum, learners introduced themselves to their colleagues and to the instructor. In "Frequently Asked Questions," they asked about how to find course materials on the class website or use different functions on the course management system. They also clarified issues related to assignments. The "Sharing 'Almost' Anything" forum allowed the learners to discuss anything at all outside of class topics. All of the forums lent themselves specifically to the development of logistical presence and to social presence in general.

Activity Tasks

Task 1: Introduce Yourself to the "Getting to Know You" Forum

- Review the guidelines posted on the "Getting to Know You" forum to make sure your introduction includes any specific information requested by the instructor.

- Post an introduction on this forum. You may include background on your education, career, and family life. Include things you think may be of interest to your classmates, such as hobbies and interests. Fun facts about you may also be included. You may include a photo, audio, or video clip as well.

- During the first few days of the course, review the introductions of your classmates. What do you have in common with them? What questions or comments come to mind as you are reviewing their profiles? Respond to the introductions of your colleagues with your own comments on their profiles.

- Just as you respond to the introductions of your colleagues, other learners will be responding to your introduction. They may have additional questions for you, or comments on what they've read in your introduction. Keep these discussions going by responding to their postings.

Task 2: Review Course Content

- Browse through the information posted on the course website. This information may include the course syllabus, information on assignments, discussion forums, course policies and procedures, and institutional guidelines.

- If you have any questions about the course itself (that are not related specifically to topics to be covered in the course), post those questions in the "Frequently Asked Questions" forum.

- Check back in a day or two to find the response to your question. It may be posted by the instructor or by another learner, or both.

[handwritten: other & professor]

- You may see questions in the "Frequently Asked Questions" forum posted by other learners. If you are able to address a question, go ahead and respond. The instructor also monitors this forum, and will provide responses to questions noted here.

Task 3: Sharing "Almost" Anything

- The "Sharing 'Almost' Anything" forum is for any topic on which you wish to post. It can be anything related to the course, or something totally unrelated, such as the weather or current events on campus, in the community, or in the world, or anything in between. In this forum, you and the instructor can carry on informal conversations about any topic at all (within reason, of course).

- If you have a topic you would like to discuss with your colleagues in class that is not related to coursework, post it in the "Sharing 'Almost' Anything" forum.

- Monitor this forum throughout the course, and contribute to it as you feel appropriate.

Course Resources

- Course website
- Discussion board forums
- Postings of classmates and the instructor *[handwritten: Clarify forums - what they are, what is their purpose?]*

How Presence Was Experienced in Case 1

Table 5.1 provides an outline of the determinants of presence for Case 1. The instructor created the course website and the forums used. The instructor acted with learners as a facilitator for conversation and as an observer of, and supporter for, the process.

In this online course activity a sense of presence was created primarily through social experiences involving communication and interaction with other course participants and the instructor. It was created to a lesser degree through environmental experiences. The learners' questions about the logistics of the course resulted in interactions with the instructor and other course participants.

Presence was experienced through involvement in the course LMS. Involvement included the initiation and participation in the discussion board forums presented in the case.

Table 5.1
Determinants of Presence for Case 1

CONTENT TYPE AND FOCUS	LEARNING EXPERIENCE FORMAT	INTERACTIVE STRATEGIES	INSTRUCTOR ROLE	TYPE OF TECHNOLOGY THAT ENABLED PRESENCE	SUPPORT
Using Technology with Adult Learners: process focus	Self-paced, group-based	Discussion forums	Designer, facilitator, supporter, observer	LMS	Institutional, technical

Approaches to Knowing If Presence Was "There"

Three approaches were used to determine if presence was created as a result of this online learning activity. The LMS user progress report, transcripts of postings from these forums, and learner interaction and engagement were all examined as indicators of presence.

Learning Management System User Progress Report

It was possible to identify which learners were present in each of the three forums by examining the number and frequency of postings, taking into consideration both postings authored and postings read. This feature of the LMS was very important for the instructor to observe and be aware of nonparticipants and encourage a more active participation and sense of group presence.

Learner Engagement in Discussion

The unfolding of the creation of presence can be observed by examining the conversations built in these forums. Transcripts of learner participation in these discussion forums were evidence of their presence in class. Beginning with the initial post by a learner and continuing with responses to that initial posting and responses to those responses, the process of presence development could be viewed as it was created.

Learners and Instructor Engagement in Non-Content-Related Areas

By looking at the transcripts of postings in the beginning of the course, it was pos-

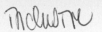 *inclusive*

sible to determine the type of presence participants engaged in. Postings included expressions of emotion, use of humor, and personal disclosure. Interactions that showed that a sense of presence was "there" included postings that followed a thread, quoted from others' messages, referred explicitly to others' messages, asked questions, complimented others, expressed appreciation, or expressed agreement. Presence was also noted through cohesive responses indicated by the use of inclusive pronouns to address the group, reference to other participants by name, and statements that were purely social, such as greetings (Schmidt & Conceição, 2008).

cohesive -inclusive pronouns + social greetings

CASE 2: SECOND LIFE® PARTICIPATION AND BLOGGING

Activity Description

This activity sought to have learners experience and reflect on the use of Second Life®, a 3-D virtual world in which learners create an avatar to represent themselves. Learners in this course became residents of this virtual world. They immersed themselves independently in simulated environments and with others in dynamic interactions.

what is this -how can I lend it

The educational organization in which the online course was offered had purchased a virtual space in Second Life®. Virtual spaces in Second Life® are called "islands," and the course had a special area within the island where learners could meet, exchange information, and chat with others. This activity involved a series of tasks that needed to be accomplished and then reported on the Blogspot website throughout the online course. This online course was composed of seven units.

Activity Tasks

Task 1: Getting Started and First Thoughts About Second Life®—Unit 1

- Review the Getting Started in Second Life® documents in the LMS and complete the tasks; watch at least two YouTube videos on Second Life®.

- Go to http://www.blogspot.com/ and select "Welcome to the Blogspot!" and then introduce yourself and share something special that you did during the holiday break. You will be posting your reflection about the Second Life® experience in this blog area.

- After you complete Blog 1: Getting Started and First Thoughts about Second Life®, post your comments on your first impressions of Second Life®: challenges in setting up your account and accessing the site, strengths of the 3-D virtual world, the most fun feature of Second Life®, and any tips you would suggest to newcomers to this virtual world.

- Ask at least one question to other course bloggers regarding their impressions of Second Life®. Respond to at least one question posted by a blogger.

Task 2: Visiting Sites and Looking for Resources—Unit 2

- In Second Life® (http://www.secondlife.com/), visit the course area and chat with whoever is online at the time you log in. Visit Second Life® during this task period as much as you can.

- In Second Life® (http://www.secondlife.com/), teleport to the following sites and look for resources in the sites available.

  - **Museum of Distance Education:** http://slurl.com/secondlife/PSU%20World%20Campus/144/13/29

  - **Penn State University World Campus:** http://slurl.com/secondlife/PSU%20World%20Campus/144/13/29

  - **Museum of Distance Education:** http://slurl.com/secondlife/Timmerman/229/9/158

  - **Memorial University 2—Distance Education and Learning Technologies (DELT):** http://slurl.com/secondlife/Memorial%20Univ%202/100/12/42

  - **Access Wisconsin** (Developed by UW-Learning Innovations, ICS, and Wisconsin Public Television): http://slurl.com/secondlife/Access Wisconsin/148/119/24

  - **Science Friday:** http://slurl.com/secondlife/Science Friday/219/192/28

  - **Genome Island:** http://slurl.com/secondlife/Genome/137/87/29

  - **New Media Consortium (NMC) Conference Center:** http://slurl.com/secondlife/NMC Conference Center/50/206/21

  - **Tsunami Demonstration:** http://slurl.com/secondlife/Meteora/184/37/32

  - **NOAA Virtual Island:** http://slurl.com/secondlife/Meteora/176/160/26

- **Virtual Hallucinations** (please note that this place actually lets learners know what it is like to have visual and auditory hallucinations; it can be *very* unsettling to some people): http://slurl.com/secondlife/Sedig/26/45/22
- **Nutrition Game:** http://slurl.com/secondlife/Ohio University/191/178/27
- **International Spaceflight Museum:** http://slurl.com/secondlife/Spaceport Alpha/47/77/24
- **Camp Darfur:** http://slurl.com/secondlife/Better World/175/244/21
- **Abyss Museum of Ocean Science:** http://slurl.com/secondlife/Gun/54/41/81

- Once you have completed the task, go to http://www.blogspot.com/ and select Blog 2: Visiting Sites and Looking for Resources. Then, reflect on your experience in Second Life® interacting with others, checking sites, and how you could use them as a resource.
- Ask at least one question to other course bloggers regarding their blog posting. Respond to at least one question posted by a blogger.

Task 3: Sharing Resources in Second Life®—Unit 3

- In Second Life® (http://www.secondlife.com/), visit the course area and chat with whoever is online at the time you log in. Visit Second Life® during this task period as much as you can.
- Using the search feature of Second Life®, look for resources related to online teaching and learning, instructional design, Web-based training, etc.
- Once you have completed the task, go to http://www.blogspot.com/, select Blog 3: Sharing Resources. Share at least one resource you found with the course bloggers (include the resource link to the posting). Then, describe the limitations and strengths of the resource you found and how you could use the resource. Shared resources should be unique, so before posting your resource, make sure that no one else has posted a similar one.
- Ask at least one question to other course bloggers regarding your shared resource. Respond to at least one question posted by a blogger.

Task 4: Participating in a Conference, Workshop, or Group—Unit 5

- In Second Life® (http://www.secondlife.com/), visit the course area and chat with whoever is online at the time you log in. Visit Second Life® during this task period as much as you can.

- Look for a conference, workshop, or group on the topics of Web-based training, instructional design, online teaching and learning, or related field. Participate in the event or activity for at least a week, to see developments depending on the schedule defined by the conference, workshop, or group.

- Once you have completed the task, go to http://www.blogspot.com/ and select Blog 4: Participating in a Conference, Workshop, or Group. Share the following with the course bloggers: name of the conference, workshop, or group you participated in; location in Second Life®; date of the event or activity; characteristics of the event or activity; and something new or special you learned from participating in the event or activity.

- Ask at least one question to other course bloggers regarding the conference, workshop, or group they participated in. Respond to at least one question posted by a blogger.

Task 5: Evaluating Second Life®—Unit 6

- In Second Life® (http://www.secondlife.com/), visit the course area and chat with whoever is online at the time you log in. Visit Second Life® during this task period as much as you can.

- Go to http://www.blogspot.com/, select Blog 5: Evaluating Second Life®. Post your last blog including: comments on the format of Second Life® and how you navigated through the virtual world, suggestions on how Second Life® can be used other than the way it was used in this course, how successful you were in Second Life®, how worthwhile the virtual experience was—and what criteria you used to make this judgment, and strengths and weaknesses of Second Life®—and what criteria you used to make these judgments.

Resources

- Second Life®: http://www.secondlife.com/
- Video tutorials: http://adminstaff.vassar.edu/sttaylor/SL-Tutorials
- Finding events: http://sl.nmc.org/wiki/SLED_Calender
- Blogspot: http://www.blogspot.com/

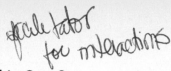
facilitator for interactions (handwritten)

How Presence Was Experienced in Case 2

Table 5.2 outlines the determinants of presence for Case 2. The instructor designed the activities, participated as a facilitator for interactions, assessed learners' experiences and provided feedback, and provided instructional and technical support on the use of Second Life® and the Blogspot website.

In this online course activity a sense of presence was created through social and environmental experiences. Social experiences involved communication and interaction with course participants, instructor, and other people in the virtual world. Environmental experiences encompassed the learners' reflections and feedback about the virtual world in the blogging portion of the activity.

Presence was experienced through immersion in the virtual world and involvement through blogging. Immersion in this online course occurred through learner visits to simulated environments; synchronous meetings with the instructor and other learners in the course area of Second Life®; and participation in a conference, workshop, or group event. Learners became involved through blogging and during Second Life® synchronous interactions. *synchronous group events* (handwritten)

Approaches to Knowing Presence Was "There"

Three approaches were used to determine if presence was created: transcripts of postings in the blog area, participation in synchronous meetings in Second Life®, and mid-course feedback.

CONTENT TYPE AND FOCUS	**LEARNING EXPERIENCE FORMAT**	**INTERACTIVE STRATEGIES**	**INSTRUCTOR ROLE**	**TYPE OF TECHNOLOGY THAT ENABLED PRESENCE**	**SUPPORT**
Using Technology with Adult Learners: process focus	Self-paced, group-based	Virtual world experience, blog posting, e-office hours	Designer, facilitator, evaluator, supporter	Second Life®, Blogspot	Instructional, technical

Table 5.2
Determinants of Presence for Case 2

Transcripts of Postings   The tasks for this online activity encouraged learners to share their experiences in Second Life® in the Blogspot environment. Blog transcripts provided rich information about learners' feelings on the new technology and how they were communicating and interacting with others. It was possible to see how often and how many postings learners created in the Blogspot website. This online activity allowed them to help each other through navigating the 3-D world, avoiding inappropriate behavior in Second Life®, and sharing new resources. The sharing and helping encouraged a sense of group presence.

Synchronous Meetings in Second Life®   Learners had the option to meet once a week in Second Life® with the instructor and other learners. These meetings served as electronic office hours where they could clarify concerns, share new learning, and meet with other people in Second Life® who happened to be joining the group at the time of the meeting. The number of learners participating in the synchronous meetings varied from week to week. The meetings created a sense of group presence.

Mid-Course Feedback   Learners were asked to complete a mid-course feedback survey posted in the course management system. This survey was anonymous. Learners were asked if they found their experiences with Second Life® to be useful and also asked to comment on their feelings about their experiences. In addition, they were invited to share and comment on whether the blogging exercises were helpful to them.

CASE 3: CREATING A WEB-BASED TRAINING COURSE AS A TEAM

Activity Description

This team-based online activity involved the creation of a Web-Based Training (WBT) course for adult learners from the development of a Design Document to the placement of the course in the learning management system. Each team was involved in completing eight tasks collaboratively throughout the course. Each task helped each team develop and design the WBT. The final product was a learning management system course website with content, instructional strategies, assessment strategies, and so on. This online activity took place during the entire course, but most interesting is how it was conducted at the end of the course.

Activity Tasks

Task 1: Design Document—Unit 1

• Develop organization background and learners' characteristics.

Task 2: Design Document—Unit 2

• Develop course goal and objectives.

Task 3: Design Document—Unit 3

• Develop instructional strategies, navigation map or outline, and resources.

Task 4: Design Document—Unit 4

• Develop project management, deliverables, project flow chart, unit storyboards.

Task 5: Presentation of Design Document—Unit 5

• Present Design Document in the learning management system.

Task 6: Design Course in Learning Management System—Unit 6

• Place course materials in the learning management system, including handouts, PowerPoint files, instructions on how to navigate through the website, strategies and assessments, and so on.

• Provide storyboards in a PowerPoint format as the final product.

Task 7: WBT Rapid-Prototype Evaluation—Unit 7

• Evaluate the website individually using the learning management system prototype form.

Task 8: WBT Presentation—Course Wrap-Up

• Present the WBT in its final form in the learning management system for the entire class to view and comment.

End-of-the-Online-Course Evaluation Activity

This online activity evaluation was based on three components: (1) Design Document, (2) WBT final project presentation, and (3) team evaluation. The Design Document and final project presentation were graded by the instructor; the team project was graded by course participants. Following are the grading criteria for each component.

1. Design Document

[handwritten: what does this mean]

- Content should be comprehensive and appropriate.

- Document should include introduction, instructional strategy, flow chart, storyboards, resources, project management, and deliverables. Elements should be described in detail.

- Document should be well organized and flow in a logical pattern. Elements of the document should be aligned with each other, i.e., instructional strategies are in alignment with course objectives.

[handwritten: what are rules of thumb for this?]

- Clarity of communication style of the document should be clearly written, that is, for a third-party reader.

- Quality of writing should be free of typos, misspellings, and so on.

2. WBT Final Project

- *Instructional design:* Objectives should be clear, units should provide the skills and knowledge required to master the objectives, structure of the units should be clear and easy to follow, units should include assessment strategies that are in alignment with unit objectives, and language used to present the units should be clear and easy to understand.

[handwritten: how is this done? Does moodle do this]

- *Clarity of directions and interactions:* It should be easy to navigate the units; icons, links, and buttons should clearly relate to their functions; directions related to sending the instructor e-mail should be clear; hypertext links should provide relevant and valuable information; user should be able to return easily to the units from a hypertext link; and directions to access the threaded discussion should be clear.

- *Writing:* Of course documents should be free of typos, misspellings, and so on.

3. Team Project Evaluation

- The team project was graded based on self-evaluation and evaluation of each team member according to the following criteria:

  - *Intellectual contributions:* a team member's contribution to the content of the project.

  - *Logistical contributions:* posting, typing, editing, presenting, uploading, and so on.

  - *Creative contributions:* to the design of the project.

  - *Leadership contributions:* the driving force behind the operation at one time or another during the project.

- Part of the grading activity was to provide comments to substantiate the evaluation points.

How Presence Was Experienced in Case 3

Table 5.3 outlines the determinants of presence for Case 3. The instructor designed the activities, observed the team process, assessed learners' experiences and provided feedback, and provided instructional and technical support on the use of the learning management system and on how to create a Web-based course.

Table 5.3
Determinants of Presence for Case 3

CONTENT TYPE AND FOCUS	LEARNING EXPERIENCE FORMAT	INTERACTIVE STRATEGIES	INSTRUCTOR ROLE	TYPE OF TECHNOLOGY THAT ENABLED PRESENCE	SUPPORT
Using Technology with Adult Learners: product focus	Group-based	Team project	Designer, observer, supporter, evaluator	LMS	Instructional, technical

In this online course activity, a sense of presence was created through social and environmental experiences. Social experiences involved communication and interaction among course participants and the instructor. Environmental experiences were based on learners' feedback about the learning management system environment while developing the WBT course project.

Presence was experienced through realism. Realism occurred through learners' involvement in a real-life team experience in which they developed a WBT product. During course orientation, learners assigned team roles (instructional designer, team manager, graphic designer, and so on) to be played throughout the course as the project tasks were accomplished. Learners participated in active discussions to accomplish project tasks in the team discussion area and presented each task to the whole class (involvement). During this process, learners imagined that they were working as a real-world team, playing the various roles, and developing a real-life product.

Approaches to Knowing If Presence Was "There"

Three approaches were used to determine if presence was felt in this course: learning management system user progress report, learner engagement in team project discussions, and self- and team evaluation at the end of the course.

Learning Management System User Progress Report It was possible to identify which learners were present and when during the team project process based on their number of postings, frequency of access, postings authored, and postings read. This feature of the LMS was very important in allowing the instructor to observe nonparticipants and encourage a more active participation and sense of team presence.

Learner Engagement in Team Project Discussions A special forum area was set up for each team and in each of these areas topics were created for each task. Learners' transcripts of their participation were a clear evidence of their presence in the team project process. Team project discussions focused on the accomplishment of the tasks. Learners participated in these discussions asynchronously via the LMS and in some cases synchronously via the chat feature. These interactions created a sense of team presence.

Self- and Team Evaluation at the End of the Course This online activity culminated in a combined self- and team evaluation. This evaluation was submitted only to the instructor with insightful information about team presence. Each person had to provide detailed comments on each team member's participation in the project process. Participants commented on their perceptions of others' intellectual, logistical, creative, and leadership contributions. This was not only a team project activity but also a way for the instructor to know how learners were experiencing presence during the team project process.

CREATING A SYLLABUS WITH A SENSE OF PRESENCE

This book has presented the Being There for the Online Learner model and the framework for designing online courses with a sense of presence. In Appendix 3 we will offer you a sample syllabus that incorporates the case examples addressed in this chapter. The course syllabus can serve as a template for you with detailed course activities that provide a sense of presence. The orientation materials and welcome letter, as described in Chapter 4 and addressed in Case 1 of this chapter, can be separate documents or included in the syllabus. In the course outline section of the syllabus, you can see when the orientation takes place and the order of the activities and assignments.

The course syllabus can serve as the contract between the instructor and the learner. It presents the big picture. The course outline is a snapshot of the course process. You may also want to provide detailed information about each unit, so that learners can focus on one unit at a time to better manage the course assignments.

FINAL THOUGHTS AND FUTURE DIRECTIONS

What is happening in the field of online teaching and learning today that makes a sense of presence so important? Why is creating a sense of presence so necessary in online environments? How can a sense of presence be created for online teaching and learning? In Chapters 1 and 2 we discussed how technology is ubiquitous today and has become an integral part of our lives. Information and knowledge are now in the palms of our hands; we can access them through the tips of our fingers. Just having and accessing information in a casual way, however, does not necessarily mean we are learning. Learning—the process of making sense of information and constructing and applying knowledge in formal online settings—requires a different way of thinking, feeling, and behaving.

Our intention in this book was to make you aware of what makes teaching face-to-face and teaching online distinctive. The basic difference is the separation of the instructor from the learners and the learners from each other. This separation can cause feelings of isolation, frustration, and anxiety. A way to overcome these feelings in the online environment is through an awareness and understanding of a sense of presence.

As you have seen throughout our book, the sense of presence doesn't just naturally happen. It is the result of awareness, understanding, intentional planning and design, and involvement through experience on the part of the instructor. It is also the awareness and active involvement on the part of the learners. But these are not all. In the online teaching-learning experience, everyone must also think, feel, and behave with a sense of presence.

The concept of presence is elusive. It is not an easy thing to be aware of or understand in the online environment. Presence requires the "other." We are social beings and tend to want to be present with others. When we do not have this sense of presence we feel isolated and seek ways to overcome isolation. Being social is part of our perceptual process in both the real world and the virtual space. It is through this perceptual process that we make sense of presence by interacting with information and others in the online environment. This process requires the dynamic interplay of thought, emotion, and behavior, between the private world and the shared world, and it occurs at the subconscious level. Even though we interact with others, we continuously go through this process in the online environment from an individual point of view.

In addition to being aware of a sense of presence from an individual point of view, it is critical that we understand the social, psychological, and emotional aspects of presence and ways in which they influence participants' interactions in the online environment. Although most research focuses on cognitive, social, and teaching presence, this book considers them using a perceptual systems approach as central to the design process. It introduces you to the Being There for the Online Learner model. This model incorporates the types of experience, modes of presence, and dimensions of the learner as a representation of the perceptual process in the online environment.

We introduced you to the framework for designing online courses with a sense of presence in order to help you think in a more concrete way about the abstract concept of presence. We hope this framework will serve as a systematic guide to help you intentionally plan for and design your online course with a sense of presence. No matter if you are a new or an experienced online instructor, the suggestions in this book should assist you in rethinking or reshaping your instruction. Involvement through experience will allow you to apply the concepts of our book in your ongoing practice.

Research on the concept of presence needs to be expanded to enhance the field of online education. There have been attempts to clearly define the concept of presence (Kehrwald, 2008), refine the community of inquiry framework (Garrison & Arbaugh, 2007), broaden the concept of presence by including the context (Gunawardena, 1995; Gunawardena & Zittle, 1997), and identify ways to measure presence (Biocca, Burgoon, Harms, & Stoner, 2001). New areas related to online presence that can add to the research and practice knowledge base may include the application and testing of our model and framework from an instructor and learner perspective, case studies that apply our design framework, techniques for measuring online presence, and strategies used by instructors to balance their online workload when creating a sense of presence.

As technology continues to evolve, we are no longer limited to physical interactions; we connect with others worldwide, our world becomes smaller, and the boundaries between the real and the virtual dissolve. In this new era of rapid technological advances, the value of creating a sense of presence cannot be ignored. How do you know if you are here or there? Remember, making sense of presence in the online environment is how you think, feel, and behave in "being there" and "being together" with others.

RESOURCE	DESCRIPTION
Bower, B., & Hardy, K. (Eds.). (2005). *From Distance Education to e-Learning: Lessons Along the Way.* New Directions for Community Colleges. San Francisco: Jossey-Bass.	This resource looks at the current challenges and successes of faculty, learner support staff, and administrative leaders as they endeavor to create a quality learning environment through distance education. It also addresses current unresolved issues and some looming on the horizon.
Conceição, S.C.O. (Ed.). (2007). *Teaching Strategies in the Online Environment.* New Directions for Adult & Continuing Education. San Francisco: Jossey-Bass.	This resource provides an overview of the process by which online courses are designed and explains how online teaching strategies can be suited to the adult learner. Targeted to the novice teacher, each chapter in the volume provides useful ways of thinking about teaching online and transferring instructional strategies from the face-to-face classroom to the online environment.
Conrad, R., & Donaldson, J. A. (2005). *Engaging the Online Learner: Activities and Resources for Creative Instruction.* San Francisco: Jossey-Bass.	This book provides an innovative framework that helps instructors convert course materials and become more involved as knowledge generators and cofacilitators of a course. It also provides specific ideas for test activities.

Continued

RESOURCE	DESCRIPTION
Palloff, R., & Pratt, K. (2003). *The Virtual Learner: A Profile and Guide to Working with Online Learners.* San Francisco: Jossey-Bass.	This is an essential resource for online educators working with learners in higher education and training settings. The book provides an overview of key issues in online learning and covers a broad range of topics, including learning styles, multicultural issues, evaluation, retention, and the challenging problems of plagiarism and cheating.
Palloff, R., & Pratt, K. (2008). *Assessing the Online Learner: Resources and Strategies for Faculty.* San Francisco: Jossey-Bass.	This hands-on resource helps higher education professionals understand the fundamentals of effective online assessment. It offers guidance for designing and implementing creative assessment practices tied directly to course activities to measure learning.
Shank, P. (Ed.). (2006). *Online Learning Idea Book.* Aurora, Colorado: Learning Peaks.	The author and her colleagues offer hundreds of examples that demonstrate why technology doesn't build interactive learning; creative thinking and good, solid instructional design does.
Shank, P., & Sitze, A. (2004). *Making Sense of Online Learning: A Guide for Beginners and the Truly Skeptical.* Aurora, Colorado: Learning Peaks.	This practical primer will help you understand how online learning technologies work and how they fit into your organization. You'll gain good knowledge of design, infrastructure, and evaluation, as well as the confidence to make informed decisions. The book is supported with a dedicated website: www.learningpeaks.com/msoll/
Smith, R. (2008). *Conquering the Content: A Step-by-Step Guide to Online Course Design.* San Francisco: Jossey-Bass.	This resource provides a practical blueprint for course development and content presentation for Web-based courses, offering online instructors practical templates, learning guides, and sample files with which to construct and manage course content.

APPENDIX 2: ONLINE COURSE DESIGN RESOURCES

RESOURCE	DESCRIPTION
Boettcher, J., & Conrad, R. (2010). *The Online Teaching Survival Guide: Simple and Practical Pedagogical Tips.* San Francisco: Jossey-Bass.	This practical guide focuses on the life of a course and provides tips to help readers through each phase of it.
Comeaux, P. (Ed.). (2002). *Communication and Collaboration in the Online Classroom: Examples and Applications.* San Francisco: Jossey-Bass.	The contributing authors of this collection of essays explain and analyze the ways in which they have incorporated interactive technologies into their instructional practices, providing readers with a frame for understanding the relationships between technology and the learning process.
Finkelstein, J. E. (2006). *Learning in Real Time: Synchronous Teaching and Learning Online.* San Francisco: Jossey-Bass.	A valuable resource for those wanting to humanize and improve interaction in their online courses by adding a synchronous learning component, this book guides instructors in evaluating how and when to use it and illustrates how educators can develop their own strategies and styles.

Continued

RESOURCE	DESCRIPTION
Hanna, D., Glowacki-Dudka, M., & Conceição-Runlee, S. (2000). *147 Practical Tips for Teaching Online Groups: Essentials for Web-Based Education.* Madison, WI: Atwood Publishing.	This comprehensive collection of strategies for teaching effectively online begins with preinstruction preparation, progressing through actual online teaching. The book will help you feel more comfortable and competent as you create your online course. It addresses popular myths in online education and also anticipates problems you may face teaching in the online environment.
Lehman, R., & Berg, R. (2007). *147 Practical Tips for Synchronous and Blended Technology Teaching and Learning.* Madison, WI: Atwood Publishing.	Drawn from years of experience and grounded in distance-learning research, the tips included here are placed in the respected framework of the instructional design process: preplanning, planning, developing, implementing, and evaluating.
Palloff, R. M., & Pratt, K. (2004). *Collaborating Online: Learning Together in Community.* San Francisco: Jossey-Bass.	This book provides practical guidance for faculty seeking to help their learners work together in creative ways, move out of the box of traditional papers and projects, and deepen the learning experience through their work with one another.
Palloff, R. M., & Pratt, K. (2007). *Building Online Learning Communities: Effective Strategies for the Virtual Classroom.* San Francisco: Jossey-Bass.	This hands-on guide explores the development of virtual classroom environments that foster a sense of community and empower learners to take charge of their learning to successfully achieve learning outcomes.
West, J. A., & West, M. L. (2008). *Using Wikis for Online Collaboration: The Power of the Read-Write Web.* San Francisco: Jossey-Bass.	This book focuses on using wikis in collaborative and constructivist learning. It provides pedagogical background and practical guidelines, tools, and processes and supports the effective design and delivery of online courses through the integration of collaborative writing and design activities.

COURSE NAME
SEMESTER, YEAR

Instructor name:

Phone number:

E-mail:

Web page:

Skype ID:

Twitter:

Office location:

Office Hours

Second Life® office hours:

Electronic office hours:

Table of Contents

Second Life® Participation and Blogging

Team Project

Course Requirement Percentages

Grading Scale

Special Notes

Course Outline

COURSE DESCRIPTION

Insert here a detailed description of the course.

COURSE OBJECTIVES

Upon completion of this course, it is expected that participants will be able to:

1.

2.

3.

INSTRUCTIONAL MATERIALS

Textbooks: required and recommended

WEBSITE RESOURCES

Mail and calendar system:

Learning management system (LMS):

COURSE REQUIREMENTS

Course requirements include: (1) online discussions, (2) Second Life® participation and blogging, and (3) team project.

Online Discussions

The course is divided into units during which specific readings are assigned. You will be expected to complete reading assignments and participate actively in online discussions.

You will be required to post at least **three** (quality) messages per week. For each online discussion unit, two class members will be assigned specific roles to facilitate discussion and to summarize discussions. These roles include:

Facilitator   As the facilitator, you are responsible for initiating the discussion with one or two questions from the readings. As class members respond to your questions, the facilitator extends the discussion by posing new questions on issues that arise out of the discussion. Additionally, the facilitator may refer back to the readings to initiate discussion on another aspect of the topic. Facilitators are responsible for selecting discussion topics based on the readings, setting an agenda for the length of the discussion period, providing brief summaries during the discussion and initiating new topics, and keeping an active and involved discussion going throughout the specified online discussion dates.

Note: Facilitators are also contributors. You must post the minimum postings required per week in addition to facilitating the discussion. Summary should be posted in the LMS on the last day of the unit.

Summarizer   As the presenter of the summary, you are responsible for summarizing the discussion and providing all members with a brief review of the main issues, key points that participants made, and any conclusions that the group made. This summary should be posted in the group's conference area on the last day of the unit period and should be no more than two to three paragraphs in length. Summaries may be descriptive (based on individual contributions, weekly contributions, discussion themes, or facilitator questions), comparative (based on discussions addressing pros/cons, agreements/disagreements, and comparisons among concepts), process-based (explaining the group process during the discussion), or a combination of two or more formats.

Note: Summarizers are also contributors. You must post the minimum postings required per week in addition to the summary.

Contributor   During online discussions, you are required to respond to questions posted by your group members, as well as review and comment on the responses of others through the discussion board indicating the name of your group. These online discussions will provide an opportunity for you to analyze some of the main concepts in the readings and other current literature and extend your knowledge through interaction with your group.

Note: Each response must clearly tie back to the reading materials and/or course content. Participants post comments in a variety of formats. Some introduce scholarly references from other sources to support or highlight their perspectives. Others discuss personal experiences. Still others bring in professional experiences. Any of these formats are acceptable, but each response must refer back to a point or points in the material. Participants should be able to make their arguments, describe experiences, or discuss alternative perspectives within the context of the material. Therefore, each comment should explicitly connect with some aspect of the readings.

Helpful hints for posting:

• Use names

• Repeat what others say to indicate understanding (online empathy)

• Admit trouble or lack of understanding, if that is the case

• Ask questions

• Sign your posting

ONLINE DISCUSSIONS CRITERIA	POINTS
Role playing (requirements of assigned role are filled): Post a minimum of 3 messages per week. Role: Facilitator, Summarizer, and/or Contributor. *Note:* Facilitators and summarizers are also contributors. You must post the minimum postings required per week in addition to facilitating and summarizing the discussion.	3
Critical thinking (demonstrate evidence of dynamic reorganization of knowledge in meaningful and usable ways): *Analysis:* Identify main ideas in readings; differentiate core ideas from supporting information; and give detail and use language that demonstrates an understanding of the major concepts. *Evaluation:* Assess information for its reliability and usefulness; discriminate between relevant and irrelevant information; determine how information can be applied in real-life; and recognize fallacies and errors in reasoning (vagueness, untruths, etc.). *Connection:* Compare/contrast similarities and differences between concepts; infer unknown generalizations or principles from information or observations; use generalizations and principles to infer unstated conclusions about specific information or situations; identify causal relationships between events or objects.	3
Total points (6 points per discussion; 30 points total)	6

Second Life® Participation and Blogging

The purpose of this activity is for learners to experience and reflect on the use of Second Life®, a 3-D virtual world, in which learners create an avatar to represent themselves. Learners in this course become the virtual world's residents. In this virtual world, learners immersed themselves independently in simulated environments and with others in dynamic interactions.

Using an area of Second Life® island designated for the course, exchange information, and chat with others. This activity involves a series of tasks that need to be accomplished and then reported on the Blogspot website throughout the online course.

Tasks

Task 1: Getting started and first thoughts about Second Life®—Unit 1

Task 2: Sharing resources in Second Life®—Unit 2

Task 3: Visiting sites and looking for resources—Unit 3

Task 4: Participating in a conference, workshop, or group—Unit 5

Task 5: Evaluating Second Life®—Unit 6

Resources

- Second Life®: http://www.secondlife.com/
- Video tutorials: http://adminstaff.vassar.edu/sttaylor/SL-Tutorials
- Finding events: http://sl.nmc.org/wiki/SLED_Calender
- Blogspot: http://www.blogspot.com/

BLOG 1: Getting Started and First Thoughts about Second Life®

SECOND LIFE® PARTICIPATION AND BLOGGING CRITERIA	POINTS
Complete orientation activities in Second Life®. Post the introductory message.	2
Blog 1 reflection is comprehensive (includes comments on challenges in setting up account and accessing the site, strengths of the 3-D virtual environment, most fun feature of Second Life®, and any tips to newcomers to this virtual environment). Ask at least one question to other bloggers regarding their impressions of Second Life® and respond to at least one question posted by a blogger. Contributions indicate a level of critical perspective and analysis.	2
Total points (4 points per blog; 20 points total)	4

BLOG 2: Sharing Resources in Second Life®

SECOND LIFE® PARTICIPATION AND BLOGGING CRITERIA	POINTS
Visit the course area in Second Life® and chat with whoever is online at the time of the log in. Teleport to the sites posted by the instructor.	2
Blog 2 reflection is comprehensive (includes comments on experience in Second Life® interacting with others, checking sites, and suggesting how the sites could be used as a resource for the development of the Web-Based Training program). Ask at least one question to other bloggers regarding their blog posting and respond to at least one question posted by a blogger. Contributions indicate a level of critical perspective and analysis.	2
Total points (4 points per blog; 20 points total)	4

BLOG 3: Visiting Sites and Looking for Resources

SECOND LIFE® PARTICIPATION AND BLOGGING CRITERIA	POINTS
Visit Second Life® and chat with whoever is online at the time of the log in. Look for resources in Second Life® related to online teaching and learning, instructional design, Web-based training, etc.	2
Blog 3 reflection is comprehensive (includes the link to the site visited, comments on at least one resource found in Second Life®, description of limitations and strengths of the resource and how it could be used in the development of a Web-Based Training program, and comment on the uniqueness of the resource). Ask at least one question to other bloggers regarding the shared resource and respond to at least one question posted by a blogger. Contributions indicate a level of critical perspective and analysis.	2
Total points (4 points per blog; 20 points total)	4

BLOG 4: Participating in a Conference/Workshop/Group

SECOND LIFE® PARTICIPATION AND BLOGGING CRITERIA	POINTS
Look for a conference, workshop, or group on the topics of Web-based training, instructional design, online teaching and learning, or related field in Second Life®. Participate in the event or activity for at least a week to see developments depending on the schedule defined by the conference, workshop, or group.	2
Blog 4 reflection is comprehensive (includes name of the conference, workshop, or group; location in Second Life®; date of the event or activity; characteristics of event or activity; and something new or special learned from participating in the event or activity). Ask at least one question to other bloggers regarding the conference, workshop, or group participated in and responded to at least one question posted by a blogger. Contributions indicate a level of critical perspective and analysis.	2
Total points (4 points per blog; 20 points total)	4

BLOG 5: Evaluating Second Life®

SECOND LIFE® PARTICIPATION AND BLOGGING CRITERIA	POINTS
Visit Second Life® and chat with whoever was online at the time of log in.	2
Blog 5 reflection is comprehensive (includes comments on the format of Second Life® and how it was navigated, suggestions on how Second Life® could be used other than the way it was used in this course, how successful you were in Second Life®, how worthwhile the virtual experience was and what criteria you used to make this judgment, and strengths and weaknesses of Second Life® and what criteria used to make this judgment). Contributions indicate a level of critical perspective and analysis.	2
Total points (4 points per blog; 20 points total)	4

Team Project

This assignment involves the creation of a Web-Based Training (WBT) course for adult learners from development of a Design Document to the placement of the course in the LMS. Each team will be involved in completing eight tasks collaboratively throughout the semester. Each task will help the team to develop and design the WBT. The final product will be a course site with content, instructional strategies, assessment strategies, and so on.

TASKS	DUE DATE
Task 1: Design Document Organization background, learner characteristics	
Task 2: Design Document Course goal, course objectives	
Task 3: Design Document Instructional strategies, navigation map/outline, resources	
Task 4: Design Document Project management, deliverables, project flow chart, and unit storyboards	
Task 5: Presentation of Design Document	
Task 6: Course: Placement of course materials in the LMS, including handouts, PowerPoint presentation, instructions on how to navigate through the site, strategies and assessments, etc.) Storyboards should be in a PowerPoint format.	
Task 7: WBT rapid-prototype evaluation: Group members will evaluate the site individually using a rapid-prototype form.	
Task 8: Program/course presentation in the LMS and for the class	

Team and Self-Evaluation

The team project will be graded based on two aspects: (1) team and self-evaluation, and (2) instructor evaluation.

Team project evaluation consists of:

- Evaluation of every member in your group on the following criteria:

  - Intellectual contributions (an individual's contribution to the content of the educational program)

  - Logistical contributions (posting, typing, editing, presenting, etc.)

- Creative contributions to the design of the educational program
- Leadership contribution (i.e., being the driving force behind the operation at one time or another)

- Evaluation of your personal contribution/performance to the team.
- Comments to substantiate the evaluation points.

TEAM AND SELF-EVALUATION	POINTS
Scale: 1–5 with 5 high contribution, 1 low contribution.	
Intellectual contributions	5
Logistical contributions	5
Creative contributions	5
Leadership contributions	5
Total points (points will be averaged)	20

Instructor Evaluation

DESIGN DOCUMENT	
Content: Comprehensiveness, appropriateness, and quality. Document includes all the elements of the assignment: introduction, instructional strategy, flow chart, storyboards, resources, project management, and deliverables. Elements are described in detail.	7
Organization: Document is well organized and flows in a logical pattern. Elements of the document are in alignment with each other; instructional strategies are in alignment with course objectives.	3
Clarity of communication style: The document is clearly written even for a third-party reader.	2
Quality of writing: Grammar, syntax, and spelling are correct; the document is free of typos, misspellings, etc.	3
Total points	**15**

WBT FINAL PROJECT

Instructional design: (1) Objectives are clear; (2) units provide the skills and knowledge required to master the objectives; (3) structure of the units is clear and easy to follow; (4) units have assessment strategies that are in alignment with unit objectives; and (5) language used is clear and easy to understand.	5
Clarity of directions and interactions: (1) It is easy to navigate the units; (2) icons, links, and buttons clearly relate to their functions; (3) directions related to sending the instructor e-mails are clear; (4) hypertext links provide relevant and valuable information; (5) user is able to return easily to the units from a hypertext link; (6) directions to download the plug-in are clear and easy to follow; and (7) directions to access the threaded discussion are clear.	7
Quality of writing: Grammar, syntax, spelling are correct; documents are free of typos, misspellings, etc.	3
Total points	**15**

COURSE REQUIREMENT PERCENTAGES

REQUIREMENTS	POINTS
Online discussions	30
Second Life® participation and blogging	20
Team project	50
Total points	**100**

GRADING SCALE

GRADE	PERCENT
A	95–100
A–	90–94
B+	87–89
B	83–86
B–	80–82
C+	77–79
C	73–76
C–	70–72

SPECIAL NOTES

In this area, include institutional information about participation by students with disabilities, accommodation for religious observations, academic misconduct, complaint procedures, appeals procedures, course incompletes, etc.

COURSE OUTLINE

DATE	UNIT	READINGS	ASSIGNMENTS	TEAM PROJECT TASKS
Week 1	**Orientation**	Second Life Tutorial	Getting-to-Know-Each-Other Survey Scavenger Hunt Second Life® Tutorial	
Weeks 2–3	**1**	Book 1: Chapters 1, 2, 3 Book 2: Chapters 1, 2	Asynchronous online discussion and summary *Blog 1: Getting Started and First Thoughts About Second Life®*	Task 1: Organization background, learner characteristics

Continued

DATE	UNIT	READINGS	ASSIGNMENTS	TEAM PROJECT TASKS
Weeks 4–5	**2**	Book 1: Chapters 4, 5, 6 Book 2: Chapters 3, 4, 5	Asynchronous Online Discussion and Summary *Blog 2: Visiting Sites and Looking for Resources*	Task 2: Course goal, objectives per unit
Weeks 6–7	**3**	Book 1: Chapters 7, 8 Book 2: Chapters 6, 7, 8, 9	Asynchronous online discussion and summary *Blog 3: Sharing Resources*	Task 3: Instructional strategies, navigation map/ outline, & resources
Weeks 8–9	**4**	Book 1: Chapters 9, 10, 11 Book 2: Chapters 10, 11, 12, 13, 14	Mid-semester evaluation Asynchronous online discussion and summary	Task 4: Project management, deliverables, project flow chart, unit storyboards
Weeks 10–11	**5**	BOOK 3 BOOK 4	Asynchronous online discussion and summary *Blog 4: Participating in a Conference/Workshop/ Group*	Task 5: Presentation of Design Document
Weeks 12–13	**6**	No readings	*Blog 5: Evaluating Second Life®*	Task 6: Creating course in the LMS
Week 14	**7**	No readings		TASK 7: WBT rapid-prototype
Week 15	**Wrap-Up**		End-of-course evaluation	TASK 8: WBT presentation

DEFINITIONS OF TERMS

Asynchronous: Participants do not need to be online at the same time. Information is posted and available to course participants on an "anytime, anywhere" basis.

Avatar: In this book, avatar refers to a character that can be personalized and used when interacting with others in the Second Life® virtual world. In this program, avatars can be created as a unique persona by incorporating hairstyles, clothes, accessories, and backgrounds.

Blog: Often used as an online journal; it can also be an online chronological publication of thoughts and Web links.

Cognitive presence: One's ability to start, create, and validate meaning through reflection and dialogue in the online environment.

Concept map: A graphical representation for organizing knowledge that shows the relationships among concepts. Concepts can be represented as boxes or circles, connected with labeled arrows in a downward-branching hierarchical structure. Relationships between concepts can be indicated by linking phrases. "Concept mapping" is the technique for visualizing these relationships among different concepts.

Determinants of presence: Components of the design process that influence the creation of presence in the online environment. These components are the type and focus of the content, the format of the learning experience, the interactive strategies implemented, the role played by the instructor, the type of technology used in the course, and the kinds of support provided.

Dimensions of the learner: They are the interior world, the interface with the real world (perception/conception process), and the concrete world shared with others.

Drop box: The drop box is a feature of some learning management system software programs that allows users to submit assignments, eliminating the need to mail, fax, or e-mail them.

Emotional presence: In this book, emotional presence is the ability to genuinely show feelings through words, symbols, and interactions with others in the online environment. In this process, learners are emotionally present when they connect with others in an authentic way during the online learning experience.

Electronic portfolio: Also known as an e-portfolio or digital portfolio, it is a collection of digital evidence gathered and managed by an online learner.

Formative evaluation: This is a method of judging the worth of an online course while the course activities are happening. It focuses on the process.

Forum: An online area used for online discussions.

Learning Management System (LMS): Web-based software for delivering, tracking, and managing online courses. It also allows users to locate learning materials and activities related to online courses from any location with Internet access.

Logistical presence: An aspect of social presence that deals with the mechanics of the online classroom. It involves learner-learner and learner-instructor interactions in non-content-related online classroom forums.

Lurkers: People who read postings in the discussion areas of an online course but rarely or never participate actively in the interactions.

Modes of presence: Ways in which we experience presence.

Online course: Instruction that is totally delivered via the Internet. Learners and instructor do not meet face-to-face.

Online environment: Communication that occurs in electronic format via the Internet.

Perceptual presence: In this book, perceptual presence is the sensory experience of "being there" and "being together" in the online environment. It involves the recognition of the online environment and actions in response to this environment. Through the perceptual process, which involves thought, emotion, and behavior, individuals interact with information and others and feel as though they are together in this learning experience.

Scavenger hunt: In online courses, a scavenger hunt is a series of tasks performed by learners during course orientation.

Second Life®: A 3-D virtual world developed by Linden Lab, launched in 2003, accessible via the Internet. This virtual world is populated by resident avatars and designed by them.

Sense of presence: In this book, a sense of presence is "being there" and "being together" with others throughout the teaching and learning experience. In this perspective, the instructor places the learner at the center of the online course development and creates the course for that learner. The instructor is accessible to the learners and the learners are accessible to the instructor and each other; and the technology is transparent to the learning process.

Social presence: One's ability to express socially and emotionally in the online environment.

Summative evaluation: A method of judging the worth of an online course at the end of the course activities. It focuses on the outcome.

Synchronous: Participants are online at the same site at the same time of day using real time technology environments, such as chat rooms.

Teaching presence: This is the ability to design, facilitate, and direct cognitive and social processes for the purposes of realizing meaningful and educational learning outcomes.

Virtual space: Refers to the online environment within which learners participate in the learning experience.

Virtual world: Refers to a computer-based simulated environment that involves

REFERENCES

Alcañiz, M., Bañoa, R., Botella, C., & Rey, B. (2003). The EMMA project: Emotions as a determinant of presence. *Psychology Journal, 1*(2), 141–150.

Argyle, M., & Dean, J. (1965). Eye-contact, distance and affiliation. *Sociometry, 28,* 289–304.

Biocca, F., Burgoon, J., Harms, C., & Stoner, M. (2001). *Criteria and scope conditions for a theory and measure of social presence.* Paper presented at the Presence 2001: Fourth International Workshop.

Brookfield, S. D. (1995). *Becoming a critically reflective teacher.* San Francisco: Jossey-Bass.

Burgess, K. R. (2007). Mentoring as holistic online instruction. In S. C. O. Conceição (Ed.), *Teaching strategies in the online environment.* New Directions for Adult and Continuing Education, no. 113 (pp. 49–56). San Francisco: Jossey-Bass.

Caspi, A., & Blau, I. (2008). Social presence in online discussion groups: Testing three conceptions and their relations to perceived learning. *Social Psychological Education, 11*(3), 323–346.

Conceição, S. C. O. (Ed.). (2007). *Teaching strategies in the online environment.* New Directions for Adult and Continuing Education, no. 113. San Francisco: Jossey-Bass.

Conceição, S. C. O., Baldor, M. J., & Desnoyers, C. A. (2009). Facilitating individual construction of knowledge in an online community of learning and inquiry through concept maps. In R. Marriott & P. Torres (Eds.), *Handbook of research on collaborative learning using concept mapping.* Hershey, PA: IGI Global.

Conceição-Runlee, S. (2001). *Faculty lived experiences in the online environment.* Doctoral dissertation. University of Wisconsin-Madison.

Cunningham, C., & Coombs, N. (1997). *Information access and adaptive technology.* Phoenix: American Council on Education and the Oryx Press.

Garrison, D. (2003). Cognitive presence for effective asynchronous online learning: The role of reflective inquiry, self-direction and metacognition. In J. Bourne & J. C. Moore

(Eds.), *Elements of quality online education: Practice and direction* (pp. 29–38). Vol. 4, Sloan C Series. Needham, MA: The Sloan Consortium.

Garrison, D., Anderson, W., & Archer, W. (2001). Critical thinking, cognitive presence, and computer conferencing in distance education. *American Journal of Distance Education*, 5(1): 7–23.

Garrison, D., Anderson, T., & Archer, W. (2003). A theory of critical inquiry in online distance education. In M. G. Moore & W. G. Anderson (Eds.), *Handbook of distance education*, 113–127. Mahwah, NJ: Erlbaum.

Garrison, D. R., & Arbaugh, J. B. (2007). Researching the community of inquiry framework: Review, issues, and future directions. *Internet and Higher Education*, 10, 157–172.

Goleman, D. (1995). *Emotional intelligence: Why it can matter more than IQ*. New York: Bantam Dell.

Gunawardena, C. N. (1995). Social presence theory and implications for interaction and collaborative learning in computer conferences. *International Journal of Educational Telecommunications*, 1(2/3), 147–156.

Gunawardena, C., & Zittle, F. (1997). Social presence as a predictor of satisfaction within a computer mediated conferencing environment. *American Journal of Distance Education*, 11(1), 8–26.

Hanna, D., Glowacki-Dudka, M., & Conceição-Runlee, S. (2000). *147 practical tips for teaching online groups: Essentials of Web-based education*. Madison, WI: Atwood Publishing.

Hargreaves, A. (2004). Emotional geographies of teaching. *Teachers College Record*, 103(6), 1056–1083.

Hawkins, R. P., & Pingree, S. (1982). Television's influence on social reality. In D. Pearl, L. Bouthilet, & J. Lazar (Eds.), *Television and behavior: Ten years of scientific progress and implications for the eighties* (pp. 224–247). DHHS Publication No. ADM 82–1196, Vol. 2. Washington, DC: U.S Government Printing Office.

Ijsselsteijn, W. A., de Ridder, H., Freeman, J., & Avons, S. E. (2000). Presence: Concept, determinants, and measurement. In *Human Vision and Electronic Imaging Conference*, proceedings of the International Society for Optical Engineering, 3959, 520–529.

Kehrwald, B. A. (2008). Understanding social presence in text-based online learning environments. *Distance Education*, 29(1), 89–106.

Krathwohl, D., Bloom, B., & Masia, B. (1964). *Taxonomy of educational objectives. Handbook II: Affective domain*. New York: David McKay.

LeDoux, J. (1996). *The emotional brain*. New York: Simon and Schuster.

Lehman, R. M. (1977). *Perceptual accommodation to the medium of television: An approach for elementary children*. Master's thesis. University of Wisconsin-Madison.

Lehman, R. M. (1991). *Perceptual interaction: A theoretical context for distance education program development/design*. Doctoral dissertation. University of Wisconsin-Madison.

Lehman, R. M. (1996). *The essential videoconferencing guide: Seven keys to success.* Madison, WI: Instructional Communications Systems.

Lehman, R. (2001). *The essential videoconferencing guide: 7 keys to success.* Madison: Instructional Communications Systems, University of Wisconsin-Extension.

Lehman, R. (2006). The role of emotion in creating instructor and learner presence in the distance education experience. *Journal of Cognitive Affective Learning (JCAL),* spring/summer issue. Available at www.jcal.emory.edu.

Lombard, M., & Ditton, T. (1997). At the heart of it all: The concept of presence. *Journal of Computer-Mediated Communication, 3*(2). Retrieved April 29, 2004, from http://www.ascusc.org/jcmc/vol3/issue2/lombard.html

Munro, J. S. (1998). *Presence at a distance: The educator-learner relationship in distance learning.* ACSDE Research Monograph 16. University Park: The Pennsylvania State University.

Noe, A. (2005). *Action in perception.* Cambridge, MA: MIT Press.

Olgren, C. (1993). *Strategies for directing your learning: A resource guide for distance learners.* Distance Education Professional Development Program. Madison: University of Wisconsin-Madison.

Palloff, R., & Pratt, K. (1999). *Building learning communities in cyberspace: Effective strategies for the online classroom.* San Francisco: Jossey-Bass.

Palloff, R., & Pratt, K. (2007). *Building online learning communities: Effective strategies for the virtual classroom.* San Francisco: Jossey-Bass.

Picard, R., Kort, B., & Reilly, T. (2004). Affective learning companion: Exploring the role of emotion in propelling the SMET learning process. Retrieved March 29, 2004, from http://affect.media.mit.edu/AC_research/lc/nsf1.html

Salovey, P., & Mayer, J. D. (1990). Emotional intelligence. *Imagination, Cognition, and Personality, 9*(3), 185–211.

Salovey P., & Sluyter, D. (1997). *Emotional development and emotional intelligence: Educational implications.* New York: HarperCollins.

Schmidt, S. W., & Conceição, S. C. O. (2008). *Logistical presence in online classrooms: Effective strategies for successful learning.* Annual Distance Teaching & Learning Conference. Madison, WI.

Sheridan, T. (1992). Musings on telepresence and virtual presence. *Telepresence. Presence: Teleoperators and Virtual Environments, 1*(1), 120–126.

Short, J., Williams, E., & Christie, B. (1976). *The social psychology of telecommunications.* London: Wiley Press.

Swan, K., & Shih, L. F. (2005). On the nature and development of social presence in online course discussions. *Journal of Asynchronous Learning Networks, 9*(3), 115–136.

Thorndike, R. L., & Stein, S. (1937). An evaluation of the attempts to measure social intelligence. *Psychological Bulletin, 34,* 275–284

Tu, C., & McIsaac, M. (2002). The relationship of social presence and interaction in online classes. *American Journal of Distance Education, 16*(3), 131–150.

Weinstein, E. A. (1969). The development of interpersonal competence. In D. A. Goslin (Ed.), *Handbook of socialization theory and research.* Chicago: Rand McNally. Available at http://jcmc.indiana.edu/vol3/issue2/lombard.html

INDEX

89; and end-of-course evaluation activity, 106–107; and questions to ask for determining presence, 90–92; and team project evaluation, 107; using information gathered from, 88–93

Experience, types of: environmental, 17–18; objective, 15–16; social, 16–17; subjective, 15

F

Facebook, 70

Feedback: e-portfolio, 71–72; instructor, 83; self- and peer, 81, 82

Finkelstein, J. E., 119

Fishbowl activity, 75

Formative evaluation, 114

Freeman, J., 5, 15, 18

From Distance Education to e-Learning: Lessons along the Way (Bower and Hardy), 117

G

Garrison, D. R., 5, 7, 8, 11, 20

Genome Island, 100

Getting to know you and your course (activity case sample 1), 95–99; approaches to knowing if presence was "there," 98; description, 95–96; determinants of presence for, 98; how presence was experienced in, 97–99; and introduction of self to "Getting to Know You" forum, 96; and learner engagement in discussion, 98; and learners and instructor engagement in non-content related areas, 98–99; and learning management system user progress report, 98; and reviewing course content, 96–97; and "Sharing

Almost Everything" forum, 97; tasks, 96–97

Getting-to-Know-You Survey, 48, 54, 56–58

Getting-to-know-your-group or -team activity, 62–64

Glowacki-Dudka, M., 14, 120

Goleman, D., 21

Group discussions, 75; learner involvement in, 86

Gunawardena, C. N., 5, 6

H

Hanna, D., 14, 120

Hardy, K., 117

Hargreaves, A., 16

Harms, C., 2, 3, 8

Hawkins, R. P., 16–17

History of philosophy course, 32

I

Ice-breakers, 60–62

Ijsselsteijn, W. A., 5, 15, 18

Immersion, 19

Individual data sheet, 68; sample, 55

Information Access and Adaptive Technology (Cunningham and Coombs), 70

Inspiration® software program, 74

Instructional presence, 72–73

Instructor: and instructor-led activities, 66–67; presence of, 11; role of, 27–28; support, mentoring, and tutoring activities for, 70–71

Interactive strategies, 27

International Spaceflight Museum, 101

Involvement, 19

K

Kehrwald, B. A., 5
Kort, B., 21
Krathwohl, D., 10

L

Learning experience, format of, 27
Learning in Real Time (Finkelstein), 119
Learning management system (LMS), 29, 44, 85; definition of, 114; user progress report, 108
LeDoux, J., 21
Lehman, R. M., 6, 7, 26, 120
Linden Lab, 115
Logical and instructional activities, 72–73
Logistical forum of group interactions, 85
Logistical presence, 72, 114
Lombard, M., 8, 9
Lurkers, 114

M

Making Sense of Online Learning (Shank and Sitze), 118
Masia, B., 10
Massachusetts Institute of Technology (MIT) Learning Companion project, 21
Mayer, J. D., 20
McIsaac, M., 5
Memorial University Distance Education and Learning Technologies, 100
Mentoring, 70–71
Munro, J. S., 3, 26
Museum of Distance Education, 100
MySpace, 70

N

National Oceanic and Atmospheric Administration (NOAA) Virtual Island, 100
Netiquette rules, 40, 53–54
New Media Consortium (NMC) Conference Center, 100
Noe, A., 7, 20
Nonmediation, illusion of, 18
Nutrition Game, 101

O

Objective experience, 15–16
Olgren, C., 26
147 Practical Tips for Synchronous and Blended Technology Teaching and Learning (Lehman and Berg), 120
147 Practical Tips for Teaching Online Groups (Hanna, Glowacki-Dudka, and Conceição-Runlee), 120
One-way instructor content presentation activities, 73
One-way learner sharing of course materials, 74
Online course, instructional design framework for: and course design task and timeline for existing course, 38; and creating online course, 37–38; determinants of presence in, 26–30; and getting learners "there" for online course, 40–41; and getting self "there" for online course, 37–40; and incorporating sense of presence in online course, 38–40; training for, 37; understanding, 30–31; using, 32–36
Online course design (Appendix 2), 119–120
Online environment, 114
Online group or team activities: facilitating, 63–64

Online Teaching Survival Guide
(Boettcher and Conrad), 119
Orientation activities, learner
participation in, 85

P

Palloff, R., x, 2, 8, 118, 120 Paper
critique activity, 79–81
Penn State University World
Campus, 100
Perceptual presence, 7, 114
Perceptual systems approach, 6, 11, 110
Picard, R., 21
Pingree, S., 16–17
Pratt, K., x, 2, 8, 118, 120
Presence, activities that create sense of:
case examples of, 95–111; before
course begins, 45–64; at end of course,
77–84; and how to know if presence is
realized, 84–93; during online course,
65–77; overview of, 43–45
Presence, determinants of: defining, 113;
examples of, for three online courses,
33; and format of learning experience,
27; and interactive strategies, 27; and
kinds of support provided, 29–30;
and role of instructor, 27; and type
and focus of content, 26–27; and type
of technology, 29; for use at end of
course, 77, 78; for use before course
begins, 45, 46; for use during course,
65–66
Presence, experience of, 13–24;
environmental, 17–18; objective,
15–16; social, 16–17; subjective, 15;
and type of experience, 15–18
Presence, modes of, 18–20; defining, 114;
and immersion, 19; and involvement,
19; and realism, 18; and suspension of
disbelief, 19–20

Presence, sense of: creating, 3–4; creating
syllabus with, 109; and creation of
online learning community, 11–12;
defining, 3, 115; emotional aspect of,
9–10; *versus* engagement, 4;
importance of understanding, 2–3;
look and feel of, 3–4; and online
environment design, 10; and online
interactions among participants,
10–11; psychological aspect of, 8–9; as
result of perceptual process, 6–7; role
of, in online environment, 1–12;
social aspect of, 8; understanding,
7–12; what is known about, 4–6
Presence, sense of, in online
environment, 25–41; and creative
writing course, 34–35; determinants
of presence for, 26–30; and examples
of determinants of presence for three
online courses, 33; and framework for
designing online courses with sense of
presence, 30–36; future of, 109–111;
and getting self "there" for online
course, 37–40; and history of
philosophy course, 32; and making
presence happen in online course, 36;
and technical project management
course, 35–36; using framework for,
32–36

R

Realism, 18
Reilly, T., 21
Rey, B., 9, 20

S

Salovey, P., 20
Scavenger hunt activity, 46–54; definition
of, 115; sample, 48–54
Schmidt, S. W., 72, 99